HOW TO WRITE A WINNING PROPO$AL

UPDATED & REVISED EDITION

By

VIRGINIA LARSON

With a special section on
Computer and Word Processing Applications
By
Charles W. Koch, Ph.D.

Published By
CLASSIC HOUSE
P.O. Box 87564
San Diego, CA 92138-7564

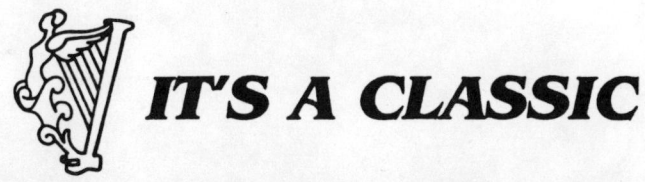

ACKNOWLEDGEMENTS

No one person writes a book such as HOW TO WRITE A WINNING PROPOSAL. The CLASSIC HOUSE staff gratefully acknowledges ideas included in this book which have been gleaned, in the course of their combined years of experience, from the motion picture and aerospace industries, from private agencies, from small and large government contractors, and from dozens of other sources. All of these sources have helped achieve the goal of the author and of the publisher: to provide a helpful, practical guide and reference for you.

Printing History

First Edition	Published 1976, ISBN # 0-88409-032-9
Revised and Updated Second Edition	Published 1986, Classic House ISBN # 0-931954-01-0 Library of Congress Catalog Card Number: 86-70729
First Printing	May, 1986
Second Printing	July, 1987

Copyright© 1986 by CLASSIC HOUSE. All rights reserved. No part of this book may be reproduced or utilized in any form or by any means, electronic or mechanical, including photocopying, recording, or by any information storage and retrieval system, without advance permission in writing from the publisher, except by a reviewer who may quote passages in a review to be used in a magazine, newspaper, or other medium of communication. Printed in the United States of America.

ISBN # 0-931954-01-0. (First Edition: ISBN # 0-88409-032-9)
Library of Congress Catalog Card Number: 86-70729

CLASSIC HOUSE

CLASSIC HOUSE is a book publisher with an impressive, versatile staff of writers, editors, and computer programmers. Members of the staff who contributed to this book are particularly knowledgeable in Proposal Planning and Preparation.

Virginia Larson, author of HOW TO WRITE A WINNING PROPOSAL, has long been a Proposal Development Specialist, as well as a technical writer and editor, and writer of other books, both fiction and nonfiction. In 1975, Larson was commissioned to write HOW TO WRITE A WINNING PROPOSAL by Sol H. Marshall, then president of the Creative Book Company and an officer in the Southern California Book Publishers Association.

In 1986, when all rights to this book were turned back to the author, CLASSIC HOUSE revised and updated HOW TO WRITE A WINNING PROPOSAL. A considerable amount of new material was incorporated, including a detailed discussion on the High-Tech use of computers and word processors in preparing today's proposals.

HOW TO WRITE A WINNING PROPOSAL is regarded as a classic in its field because of its suggested approach to proposal planning and preparation, and its practical, understandable suggestions. The book is a standard in many public libraries in the United States, and has been purchased by community organizations, teachers of Proposal Planning and Preparation, and by individuals, and business and industrial organizations who find its ideas adaptable to any type of proposal for any contract or grant project and for any proposal development staff, large or small.

It is hoped that this revised and updated Second Edition will prove equally valuable to those who purchased and used the First Edition, and that others who are being introduced to this book for the first time will find it a valuable idea and reference book.

TABLE OF CONTENTS

TITLE	Page No.
HERE'S TO YOU	1
INTRODUCTION	2
A WORD TO TOP MANAGEMENT	3
THE SIX BID DECISION QUESTIONS	5
HAVE YOU GIVEN YOURSELF THE EDGE?	6
DO YOU HAVE COMPETITIVE POWER?	7
INDUSTRIAL SECURITY	7
TYPES OF PROPOSALS	9
Unsolicited Proposals	9
Response to a Request for Proposal (RFP)	10
Sole Source Contract	10
Blanket Purchase Order	10
DOING YOUR MARKETING HOMEWORK	11
NETWORKING	12
CHANGING TIMES CHANGE METHODS	13
COOPERATIVE ARRANGEMENTS	13
Consultant Agreement	13
Teaming Agreement	14
Sample Teaming Agreement	15
PROPOSAL AND PRICING STRATEGY	16

TABLES OF CONTENTS (CONT.D)

TITLE	Page No
BUILDING A HOT PROPOSAL TEAM	17
PROPOSAL MANAGER'S JOB DESCRIPTION	18
JOB DESCRIPTIONS OF OTHER TEAM MEMBERS	21
Captain – Project Objectives and Technical Methodology	22
Captain – Project Management and Budget	22
Captain – Related Experience and Resumes	22
Proposal Pricer	23
Proposal Development Specialist	24
SUGGESTED PROPOSAL OUTLINE	25
Cover Letter	26
Introduction	27
Statement of the Customer's Project	27
Your Proposed Approach to the Project	27
Your Organization's Capabilities and Past Experience	28
Project Management Plan	28
Pricing Criteria	29
The Deliverables	29
The Realities	30
SUGGESTED PROPOSAL PLAN	31
SUGGESTED AGENDA FOR PROPOSAL KICKOFF MEETING	32
OUR FAMOUS "ROAD MAP" IDEA	33
PROPOSAL EVALUATION CRITERIA	36
580 POSSIBLE POINTS	37

TABLE OF CONTENTS (CONT'D.)

TITLE	Page No.
THE ROLE OF THE COMPUTER AND WORD PROCESSOR IN PROPOSAL PREPARATION	38
Definition of Word Processing	39
Advantages of Word Processing	39
Ease of Writing and Editing	39
Speedy Revision Cycles	39
Less Chance of Introducing New Errors When Old Errors are Corrected	40
Computerized Check of Spelling	40
More Time for the Intellectual Part of the Proposal Effort	40
Late Revisions are Possible	40
Final Proofing is Easier	40
Pitfalls of Word Processing	41
Disadvantages of "Boiler Plate"	41
Emphasis Must Be Placed on Editing	41
Computer Printers - Or, To Typeset or Not to Typeset	43
Merits and Demerits - Typescript or Typeset	43
Legibility of Typeset Copy	44
Proportional Spacing	44
More Words Per Line	44
Superior Emphasis	44
Heads Stand Out	44
Fewer Options Are Available for Typescript Copy	45
Typescript Decreases Legibility	45
Compactness	45
Two-Column Format	45
Legibility is Enhanced	45
More Words Per Page	45

TABLE OF CONTENTS (CONT'D.)

TITLE   Page No.

THE ROLE OF THE COMPUTER...(Cont'd.)

    Less Space is Squandered by "Widows"   45
    Single-Column Illustrations and   45
      Tables Can Be Used
    Omits Extra Space Between Paragraphs   45
    The Two-Column Format is Well   46
      Worth the Effort

  SUMMARY OF THE COMPUTER DISCUSSION   46

A "STORYBOARD" APPROACH TO PROPOSAL PREPARATION   47

THE MANAGEMENT REVIEW PROCESS   50

    SPECIAL NOTE TO REVIEWERS   52
    SPECIAL NOTE TO INPUTTERS   52

DETAILED SUGGESTIONS ON THE COVER LETTER AND   53
  THE INTRODUCTION

AN ATTENTION-GRABBING COVER LETTER   54

NINE "SELLING" OPENINGS FOR COVER LETTERS   55

WRITING A PERSUASIVE INTRODUCTION   57

SOME POINTS TO REMEMBER   58

YOU CAN'T WIN 'EM ALL   59

NOW, IS THIS THE END...?   60

AH, NO. IT'S JUST THE BEGINNING...   60

HERE'S TO YOU

A proposal is an attempt to persuade a business organization, a government entity, or a community service agency that you are uniquely qualified to perform a program that needs to be accomplished; that no one else can do the job as well as you.

A winning proposal, written along the guidelines suggested in this book (which has been utilized by people like you for the past decade) may sell your special, one-of-a-kind qualifications, and possibly convince your prospective customer to award you the contract or grant.

HOW TO WRITE A WINNING PROPOSAL has been updated and revised with new and innovative information and suggestions integrated with those ideas that have made this book a classic in its field.

Some ideas included here are procedures that apply to the preparation of all proposals; basic, fundamental principles you probably already know (but sometimes forget). Other ideas presented here may be new to you but can bring about:

o   New ways of thinking, or new procedures you may wish to follow.

o   New steps you can take to guarantee you will produce a responsive proposal that will favorably impress your prospective customer or funding source.

Everything that can be written about proposal planning and preparation would fill a small library; therefore, information given in this book has been carefully selected, to give you ideas that are considered to be some of the best, most useful tools. Some of the ideas, as presented, may be too grand for the size of the task on which you are bidding, but bits and pieces can be applied to help you do what needs to be done - this time.

Look on HOW TO WRITE A WINNING PROPOSAL as a wholesome salad bar or a delicious buffet. Take what appeals to you, take what you can use this time, and pass by the ideas that don't apply - this time. But, come back to the feast each time a new proposal needs to be written. Choose new ideas that will help you take a new approach with the new proposal - to take new steps toward winning the contract award, acquiring more business, receiving a vital grant, making more money.

> "Last week I didn't know how to spell
> PROPOSAL MANAGER,
> And now I are one."

This touch of irony may seem familiar. Almost everyone who has ever been involved with a proposal, at some time or another, has had this feeling of being overwhelmed by the Proposal Manager responsibility. It is hoped, this book will help reduce that feeling to a manageable level.

INTRODUCTION

Since the First Edition was published in 1976, HOW TO WRITE A WINNING PROPOSAL has been helping individuals, companies, and organizations think through the critical process of acquiring the life-blood of any enterprise:

- New business for an industrial or commercial firm, or

- Funding with dollar grants to scientific investigators and social service agencies whose missions are geared to the betterment of the human condition.

The author has been gratified to learn that this book is considered a classic in its field.

- "I can understand what the author is saying."

- "I can really use the ideas suggested here."

- "I make sure a copy of this book is always in my briefcase."

Comments like these have led to this newly updated and revised edition.

HOW TO WRITE A WINNING PROPOSAL seems to be a standard in scores of libraries throughout the country. Numerous librarians, upon meeting the author, have said:

> "This book is hard to keep on our shelves; seems as if it's always out on loan and we usually have a long waiting list. Borrowers consider this book to be a valuable reference."

If you are on a long waiting list to borrow HOW TO WRITE A WINNING PROPOSAL from your library, here's the solution to your problem: buy a copy and keep it handy for your personal use.

A WORD TO THE TOP MANAGER

As the top manager of your enterprise, you're the person responsible for planning operations and for fiscal management.

It is your responsibility to know when proposal planning and preparation should start. The proposal team needs to start work early enough to write a persuasive proposal that can be delivered on time. This could result in your winning the contract or grant award.

You must keep in mind the fact that at every step of the way, strong Management support is needed by the proposal team. They need this guidance to:

- Consistently reflect company policy in their proposal inputs.

- Integrate the agreed-upon proposal strategy.

- Keep crystal clear in their writing the technical and management approaches which have been determined by your Management group to be the best way to solve the prospective customer's problem.

- Stay on the beam.

The Management Review Cycle should be an almost continuous process, with your positive inputs being expressed in writing and then, if necessary discussed with the Proposal Manager and the individual writer.

This procedure will bring about a superior proposal, enhancing your chances of bringing in the contract.

As you contemplate correcting any weaknesses in proposal planning practices, which you consider may have lost previous contracts your organization was qualified to perform, perhaps this procedure is one you might wish to follow within the next few weeks:

Buy enough copies of HOW TO WRITE A WINNING PROPOSAL so you can give each of your key personnel a copy for personal use and ready reference. These key people would be, for example: cognizant management people, prospective technical proposal inputters, pricers, or computer and word processor specialists. After giving each person, say, a week to review the ideas that abound in this book, hold a planning meeting to discuss the future proposal activity of your enterprise.

During this planning meeting, your group should establish a written proposal Standard Operating Procedure (SOP). Lay out a plan that will go into effect automatically whenever a proposal effort looms on the horizon. You could enhance your organization's chances of winning more contract or grant awards if some of the procedures that become SOP are:

- Consideration for each proposal will start with an in-depth discussion at a Bid Decision Meeting (see next page).

- Each proposal will be written by the staff members most qualified, on the basis of technical knowledge required, and on their skill in communicating ideas.

- Staff members assigned to writing the proposal will be dedicated to the effort. (When proposal writers are placed in a position where they must "dash it off in their spare time", you get what you pay for.)

- If possible the team as a group will be co-located to an appropriate room where they can work without distractions or interruptions. (Later in this book, we'll discuss the value of cross-fertilization of ideas, etc., that this co-location makes possible.)

- Proposals will be written only if Management comes to a positive decision during the Bid Decision Meeting and is certain the organization has a realistic chance to acquire this new business.

- <u>And, finally, for your special attention because this is one of the most important SOP's, no one is allowed to sit on the RFP</u>. Within an hour after the RFP arrives at the desk of the cognizant person, be it a top management person, a contracts officer, or perhaps a program manager, the RFP should be reproduced and distributed to all possible interested parties.

  <u>How many times has someone in your organization said</u>: "I have an RFP and the proposal is due Thursday. I need help." Believe you me, that is no way to play the ball game.

On the next page is a discussion of the six key Bid Decision questions that must result in "yes" answers before your organization decides to write this proposal.

THE SIX BID DECISION QUESTIONS

1. Is this requirement in the field in which our organization has expertise?

2. Have we done our homework, to give our enterprise the competitive edge?

3. Has there been significant prior customer contact?

4. Is the proposal we plan to submit only part of our total marketing effort?

5. Are we able and willing to permit the proposal team to give a totally dedicated effort to writing the proposal?

6. Realistically, what are our chances (%) of receiving the contract? Does our marketing information tell us the job is already "wired" for another company?

REMEMBER

If you don't know about a procurement until you see it listed in the Commerce Business Daily or some other public source, it's probably too late for you to bid. But if you decide to go ahead and bid, you're in for an exciting and rewarding experience.

And, remember the first rule
of a successful sales effort:
MAKE YOUR PLAN AND WORK YOUR PLAN.

HAVE YOU GIVEN YOURSELF THE EDGE?

Pity the poor confused customer shown in the center, above. He's besieged by people wanting to do his work, wanting the money he has to spend. But pity, more, the proposer who hasn't given himself that competitive edge by doing his homework.

When we think of the danger of doing too little marketing homework, we are reminded of the clever comic strip character, "Pogo", when he paraphrased an American hero:

"We have met the enemy, and he is us."

And then there's this little ditty:

<u>He who has a thing to sell,
And goes and whispers in a well,
Is not so apt to get the dollars,
As he who climbs a hill and hollers.</u>

DO YOU HAVE COMPETITIVE POWER?

In the First Edition of HOW TO WRITE A WINNING PROPOSAL, sources were listed for city, state, and federal government contracts, and tips were given on where to obtain information on available grants to individual investigators and to organizations engaged in community service programs.

For example: The <u>Commerce Business Daily (CBD)</u> described in the First Edition, has been published by the United States Department of Commerce five days a week for many, many years. In keeping with today's High-Tech business applications, an electronic edition of the CBD is now available for computer on-line acquisition. This essential marketing tool gives such information as U.S. Federal procurement invitations, contract awards, and subcontracting leads.

However, funding policies and practices on all levels of government — in all areas of procurement — now change so rapidly we have decided in this Updated and Revised Second Edition to delete those specifics which could become obsolete tomorrow. We now leave it to you to ferret out the sources of funding based on your particular interests. If you can't think of another source, start with your public library.

> <u>As you read this book, please keep certain terminology in mind. The words "program" or "project" refer to the work the "proposal" is intended to acquire.</u>

INDUSTRIAL SECURITY

Security practices and procedures applying to proposal efforts should be as rigid as any employed to protect Department of Defense classified documents. Sound security control of the proposal effort protects your competitive posture.

Remember, your competition may be going to great lengths to find out such things as:

- Your technical approach to the customer's problem. What are your strong points...your weak points?

- Who are you teaming with?

- What is your bid price? What is your overhead figure? What are your magic numbers?

There's a joke in this business that really is not very funny. It goes like this: "We wouldn't be surprised to learn that one of our competitor's employees is moonlighting as one of our janitors. He would find our trash cans fascinating."

TYPES OF PROPOSALS

In this section is information on some of the various forms that proposals can take.

Unsolicited Proposals

This type of proposal is initiated by a business organization or social service agency and sent to a specific funding agency for consideration.

This sometimes is called "Submission on Speculation", unless your intelligence network and personal contacts with the prospective customer have determined that the agency requires the work which you have proposed performing for it. In that case, the marketing homework you have done has removed the "speculation" from your proposal effort.

These jobs may be funded as Research and Development (R&D) or Demonstration Projects, and may be designated as grants as well as contracts.

A good time to submit an unsolicited proposal is just prior to the end of the agency's fiscal year. Quite often an agency will have unexpended funds that must be committed by that time or be turned back to the appropriate government treasury.

In most cases, an unsolicited proposal is called a "letter proposal" because a two or three-page letter is all that is required to describe how you propose to perform the task.

One shouldn't sneer at "letter proposals." One company that had a five-year contract for $10 million at $2 million a year, extended that contract to ten years for $40 million. This was made possible, for the most part, because their marketing efforts continuously revealed tasks desired by the agency that could be performed for comparatively small amounts each, such as $10 thousand, or perhaps $150 thousand. Funding for these small tasks was awarded to the company as the result of a multitude of letter proposals.

Response to a Request for Proposal (RFP)

A government entity or a company, wishing to obtain detailed proposals on work to be done, often issues a Request for Proposal (RFP). In an RFP, all requirements are given in exquisite detail. Evaluators of proposals received in response to the RFP expect the proposals to respond to each requirement. A non-responsive proposal is disqualified.

Because proposals written in response to RFP's are the most complex and difficult to write, these are the proposals dealt with in detail in HOW TO WRITE A WINNING PROPOSAL.

Sole Source Contract

Despite government regulations requiring that work be made available on a competitive basis to the lowest bidder, a government agency sometimes will award a contract to a company as a "sole source". Usually, this is because the company (a contractor) has built a fine record of expertise, reliability, and dependability in the specific field of work the agency requires.

This practice is becoming less common because some of the agencies using this procurement technique wish to avoid being accused of favoritism.

To get around this charge, however, some Federal agencies will advertise the RFP in the Commerce Business Daily even though they already have decided who will receive the contract award. In the vernacular of government contracting, this means the agency has "wired" the contract to a particular company.

Your intelligence sources should let you know if the project is wired to another organization. Knowing this will save you needless expenditures of time, money, and energy.

Blanket Purchase Order

Some work required by an agency is so routine (sometimes simply procurement of contractor services such as shipment of documents, or specialist consultant services) and the agency is authorized to purchase these services from a contractor, up to a specified dollar limit for each purchase - say, $2,500 - by issuing a simple purchase order. Usually the blanket purchase order is for a specific amount of money, say, $100 thousand, which can be spent over a period of a year, but at a rate of only $2,500 at a time.

A purchase order does not require the usual review process required for a grant or a contract.

DOING YOUR MARKETING HOMEWORK

"We are all continually faced with a series of great opportunities brilliantly disguised as insoluble problems."

– John W. Gardner –

Marketing a service, like marketing a product, has numerous hazards, because of uncontrollable, unstandardized and unpredictable factors; in other words, marketing is more than just finding out who has a task you can perform and the dollars to pay you for your work.

Marketing is concerned with all the exhilerating big things, and all the other troublesome, little, routine, nit-picking chores that must be done throughout your entire organization to achieve your goal. Simple tasks that should be self-evident but are often overlooked are important. One might be: in establishing your contacts, use the telephone for voice contact, then follow up with letters of inquiry.

You must be on the alert, constantly, for needs that can be met BEST by you. Contracts are awarded to competent people; to companies with crisp management; any company with good management knows that marketing is an art the company must master.

NETWORKING

It is important to your organization to maintain a continuous intelligence-gathering function to learn about future procurements on which you can bid.

In the field of business marketing the word "networking" has become widely used to replace terms such as "seeking referrals" or "asking a satisfied customer to recommend you to another who can use your services."

Networking has replaced these other terms because the word carries the broader connotation of the function involved; it is a more descriptive term for the process that brings new business to an organization.

As an example: let's say you have a cordial relationship with a business acquaintance in the particular area of expertise that is your specialty. Routine (and frequent) conversations bring out the fact that another company has a need in your specialty. With the permission of your acquaintance, who may already be a satisfied customer of yours, you get in touch with the other potential customer, suggesting that you might be able to help meet his needs. Large contracts are gained that way.

When satisfied customers suggest your organization's name to others who need your type of services, they do this - not only because you might have asked them to do it - but because your performance on the job was so effective, so satisfying that they were glad to pass the word along. Nothing can be substituted for personal contact - even personal influence, with the decision-makers - and networking is a highly effective way to handle this.

Customer enthusiasm, generated by your organization's intentional establishment of a good public image and good public relations, plus excellent performance on a contract, with the work completed on time and within budget, is what leads to increased opportunities to bid on new work.

Changing Times Change Methods

Proposal methods and documentation preparation methods have changed drastically in the past ten years. Those of us who were around then can remember that proposals, like all other documents, were dependent upon old fashioned "cut and paste" activities. The paste pot, an Exacto knife and scissors, and a small army of typists and proofreaders who were willing to work around the clock to produce the proposal on time all were factors necessary to the person responsible for writing, producing, printing, and, perhaps, delivering, each proposal.

In addition to including new procedures that were only dreamed of when the first edition of HOW TO WRITE A WINNING PROPOSAL was published, this updated and revised edition discusses in detail the "Role of the Computer and Word Processor in Proposal Preparation." Pros and cons of the new High-Tech methods are given, and cautions are spelled out, so you won't be trapped by letting a machine do what the "little grey cells" in your brain should be doing - the thinking.

COOPERATIVE ARRANGEMENTS

Two types of cooperative arrangements should be worked out on paper in advance of proposal preparation.

Consultant Agreement

Consultant Agreement. A consultant agreement is made with an individual who is highly qualified in the technical areas of the work - perhaps a retired military officer whose retirement benefits would not be jeopardized by work done with a government contractor.

If you have an agreement _in writing_ stating that this expert is committed to work with your organization (and _only_ your organization) if the contract is awarded to you, this may then be stated in the proposal, and the expert's resume may be included. The Consultant knows it is unethical for such agreements to be executed by him with more than one organization in regard to one contract bid.

If you don't have a firm commitment from the person, you can not use the name in the proposal. The expertise reflected in the Consultant's resume may be just what the customer is looking for and could tip the scale toward you when the contract is awarded. If this Consultant is not committed with a specific agreement and, therefore, does not join to work with you on the contract, this could be interpreted by the customer as fraud on your part.

So, don't be a name-dropper hoping to snare the expert later. It usually won't work. A competitor could also figure on latching onto this expert if they win the contract award and they also could use the name in the proposal. The result is only confusion - and a serious loss of credibility.

Teaming Agreement

When you know the requirement of the RFP, if it seems necessary and valuable to the customer, work out a "Teaming Agreement" with an organization which has capabilities differing from yours in key areas required by the job. It may be necessary for you to have teaming agreements with two or three subcontractors so the total of the talents and expertise available to the customer add up to everything the customer needs to do the job.

<u>Here's a thought: Your organization may be the one to be the subcontractor to another organization which is the prime contractor. Here, again, a teaming agreement is essential</u>.

A funding agency will trust an organization whose track record is good, and will most likely respond favorably to a contractor or subcontractor with a record of well-performed, previously-funded programs.

Sample Teaming Agreement.

To clarify this proposal planning and preparation feature, following are the first few paragraphs of a sample teaming agreement:

(PROGRAM TITLE)

ABC CORPORATION - XYZ COMPANY

AGREEMENT

This agreement, made as of _____. 19___, is between the ABC Corporation and the XYZ Company and covers the cooperation of the parties in connection with the submission of a proposal by ABC to (Customer) in response to (Program Title), (RFP #123456). The parties anticipate that the contract to be awarded by (Customer) for the (Program) will be of the (Type Contract) type, and relative to such Proposal and contract agree to the following:

1. Each party will exert all reasonable effort to prepare a Proposal which will result in the selection of ABC as Prime Contractor by (Customer) and the acceptance of XYZ as a Subcontractor; and, each party agrees to continue to exert all reasonable effort toward this Proposal throughout any negotiations concerning a proposed contract or contracts which may follow the submission of such Proposal.

2. ABC will have the responsibility for the preparation, evaluation, and submission of the combined Management, Technical, Price, and Cost Proposal to (Customer). The Proposal will be submitted in the form selected by ABC with XYZ providing full assistance and advice. Each party will supply the necessary Engineering Management, Technical, and other services as well as Cost Information, Exhibits, Designs, and Plans related to the work which it proposed to perform. All contacts with (Customer) pertaining to the preparation of the Proposal will be made through ABC.

As the reader can see by these few opening paragraphs, this is a legal contract and the provisions of such a teaming agreement need to be worked out by the combined legal staffs of the organizations entering into the agreement.

PROPOSAL AND PRICING STRATEGY

Your proposal strategy and your pricing strategy depend upon what you know about the customer and the marketing environment.

For example: one company spent upwards of $100,000 preparing a proposal for a contract the company didn't have a ghost of a chance of winning. The question is asked: "How could this happen?"

- Perhaps the company was trying to invade a field in which they had had no previous experience.

- Perhaps they were pricing their proposal too low in their attempt to bring in the contract. This is a strategy known as "trying to buy in." It seldom works.

These two conditions, as well as others, can cause a "credibility gap." The customer has real doubt that a company, under such circumstances, can perform the work without running into problems related to lack of know-how and, possibly, related cost overruns.

So often, a company submitting a proposal under these conditions is disqualified almost minutes after the proposal is delivered.

Such a waste of time, and effort, and money, and morale.

BUILDING A HOT PROPOSAL TEAM

When the proposal is a large endeavor and several persons are assigned to write it, a Proposal Team should be established.

<u>First, the Proposal Manager brings to the office a large photograph of his widely-grinning face, and an adequate supply of darts</u>.

Before this hot proposal team is finished (if the Proposal Manager is good at his job) there are going to be times when they will hate his guts. Throughout the proposal effort, having darts to throw at his "obnoxious" smiling face will help relieve tension, inject an imperative sense of humor, and keep 'em going.

The Proposal Team is a special association of people, often assigned from various functional specialties, who work together to a common end, as they would on any study or program or project. If it is possible, the entire team should be co-located away from their day-to-day jobs (and telephones) to enable them to work without distractions or interruptions.

Strong leadership and direction by the <u>right</u> Proposal Manager is essential to success in getting out an effective proposal - on time. The people who head the various functional committees could be given such titles as <u>leaders</u>, <u>coordinators</u>, <u>controllers</u>, or <u>directors</u>, but for clarity, to help show the relationship of these leaders to the Proposal Manager, we choose to call them "Captains."

The following simplified organization chart gives an idea of the functions that need to be done and the relationships of all segments of the proposal team to the Proposal Manager.

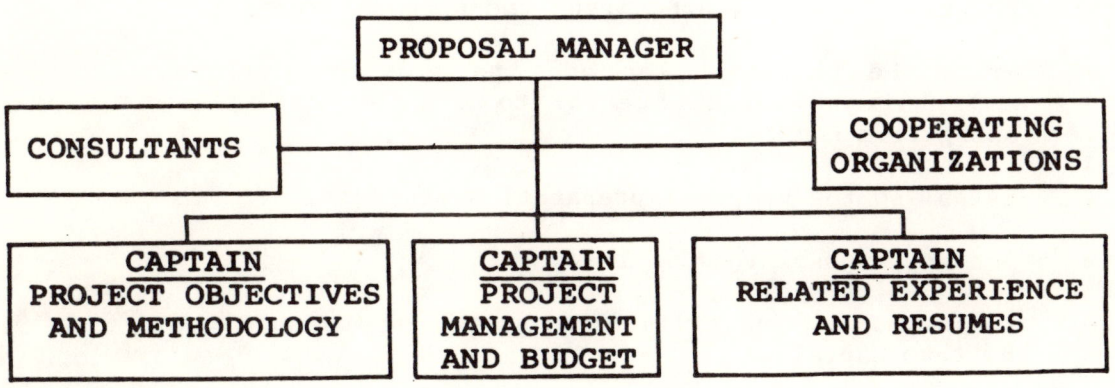

The Proposal Manager has responsibility for producing a persuasive document, so the person to be appointed to this position should have the necessary know-how. Perhaps this person is the one who knows the most about the subject of the proposal. Perhaps the Proposal Manager should be the person who is a good coordinator and organizer, or one who knows something about writing, computers, word processing, and publishing.

From the Proposal Manager's Job Description, top management will be able to determine the best person in your organization for that job. Once the Proposal Manager has been selected by Management, that person must be given the necessary responsibility, authority, and support - so the best job can be done.

<u>PROPOSAL MANAGER'S JOB DESCRIPTION</u>

The Proposal Manager provides leadership and direction for the proposal preparation work. This key person's job is to:

- Analyze the RFP to define the prospective customer's requirements.

- Do preliminary <u>project</u> planning, and define project management, organization, schedule, and budget.

- Ensure adequate planning of the proposal effort - which includes making certain that the proposal stays within the guidelines of company policies and goals.

- Recruit, organize, and direct the proposal team.

- Write the proposal plan and the proposal outline, and chair a kickoff meeting to engender enthusiasm among team members.

- Establish the proposal preparation schedule.

- Assign proposal team members.

- Review, edit, and critique proposal inputs submitted by team captains.

- Use the services of consultants (if any).

- Work with cooperating organizations (if any) to define their responsibilities in the proposed project versus your organization's responsibilities.

- Maintain continuing liaison with higher management:

    - Review the progress and results of the proposal effort.

    - Designate the personnel to be assigned to the project when the contract is awarded.

    - Obtain assistance when and where needed.

- Prepare presentation of proposal to management for review and approval

- Arrange for delivery of the proposal – on time.

The team must then be organized to write a proposal. If the team members have not previously worked together successfully, you may wish to take steps to build a team spirit. Your goals are to:

- Help members get acquainted with one another as people so they can communicate more successfully as professionals.

- Foster mutual trust.

- Build team commitment to the goals of the proposal effort.

- <u>Win</u>.

Once the group has a lively sense of itself as a team, internal communication of proposal data improves remarkably.

Obviously, if your proposal is a one-person project, this elaborate organization is not necessary, <u>but each function is necessary</u>.

As you will see from subsequent information given, if <u>you</u> are the Proposal Manager, <u>you</u> are the person who needs to know that <u>you</u> are on schedule and that <u>you</u> know where the illustrations are, and that <u>you</u> know <u>you</u> will have completed the proposal in time to deliver it on the date specified by the customer.

JOB DESCRIPTIONS OF OTHER TEAM MEMBERS

In the proposed organization chart shown earlier, the Captains are assistants to the Proposal Manager. Each Captain has certain basic responsibilities for writing and producing a section of the proposal. This key person'a job is to:

- Prepare a detailed section outline.

- Ensure that the overall proposal theme and marketing message are reflected throughout the section.

- Assign section contributors, set page limits, and establish section input due dates.

- Prepare section Introduction.

- Guide and direct individual contributors in preparation of inputs.

- Use services of consultant(s), as appropriate, and integrate inputs from cooperating organization(s).

- Assemble and review draft inputs, and participate in Management reviews as scheduled.

- Incorporate review comments into section copy.

- Ensure that final copy is ready for integration into total proposal.

The specific responsibilities of the Captains, the Proposal Pricer, and a special type of consultant - a Proposal Development Specialist - are described on the next few pages.

Captain - Project Objectives and Technical Methodology

- Responsible for describing the technical approach to the proposed project and how your organization will do the work.

Captain - Project Management and Budget

- Responsible for preparing the description of how the project will be managed, and preparing the Work Breakdown Structure (WBS) Chart or Project Evaluation Review Technique (PERT) Network Chart for the proposal.

Captain - Related Experience and Resumes

- Responsible for selecting from computer-stored paragraphs of company related experience, those items that are directly applicable to the requirements of the current RFP. The Captain then massages (slants) this information to this RFP's requirements, developing and writing additional information, if needed.

- The Captain follows the same procedure with selection of computer-stored personnel resumes, picking out those that most closely meet requirements of this RFP, and then messages the resumes to fit perfectly.

- This "personalizing" of related experience and resumes enhances your credibility for the proposal evaluators.

<u>We can't stress too strongly the need to carefully edit all of this information and slant it to this particular proposal.</u>

Proposal Pricer

The person who works out the myriad details of pricing the proposal is an integral member of the Proposal Team. This person must be privy to all of management's thinking and conversant with the strategy planned for winning this contract. How the costs are presented depends on the RFP requirements (often, a form is provided in the RFP for the proposer's use).

The company's overhead figures, however, are a matter of grave importance. This is where the company wins or loses the contract. Remember: the customer has the right to question your overhead structure during your proposal presentation. After all, he's paying for it.

Later in this book, we give details on how the customer's proposal evaluators rate a proposal. You will see, then, the important of price in their considerations as to who shall receive the contract award. The Proposal Pricer's job is to:

- Assist in overall proposal and pricing strategy.

- Assure compatibility and responsiveness of cost estimates with this RFP and its work statement.

- Work with top management and the Proposal Manager to assure approval of the proposal cost estimate by cognizant management.

- Take responsibility for the Cost Proposal.

    NOTE: The Cost Proposal usually is a document separate from the Technical and Management volume, although it is delivered with that document to provide a total package for the customer's evaluation.

As stressed in the section on Industrial Security, the Cost Proposal should be <u>held in strictest confidence within your organization</u>, with access to the information given only on a tight "need to know" basis. This is highly competitive data and needs to be carefully protected so the competition can't learn your price.

<u>Remember, if they underbid you by even
a few dollars, they could get the contract.</u>

Proposal Development Specialist

Professional consultants may be used in a proposal effort just as they are in an on-going program. The Proposal Development Specialist is considered to be a member of the newest profession. Large organizations employ teams of proposal specialists on a full-time basis and they help write the proposal as well as do much of the preliminary planning.

A small organization might use the services of a free-lance Proposal Development Specialist, who works on a short-term basis, to assist the Proposal Manager and help that key person make sure that everything that needs to be done, is done. The Proposal Development Specialist, being an outsider, usually does not write any of the technical portion of the proposal for lack of familiarity with the company's work, but this consultant can help to:

- Analyze the RFP to determine requirements, and prepare the checklist.

- Write the proposal plan.

- Prepare outlines of the technical and the management portions once these approaches have been determined by Management.

- Size the proposal, assign inputs, and suggest deadlines.

- Review, rewrite, and edit drafts, and establish format.

- Guide slanting of resumes and company experience to RFP requirements.

- Push final production to meet the customer's deadline.

SUGGESTED PROPOSAL OUTLINE

On the next few pages is a suggested proposal outline. It may not be the best outline for you to follow; quite often a careful analysis of the RFP generates a proposal outline made to order for the RFP, or, indeed, the writers of the RFP may have given you an outline which you are required to follow.

> Vision isn't enough — it must be combined with venture. It is not enough to stare up the steps — we must step up the stairs.
>
> Vance Havner

Consider this: The outline which follows is a <u>conventional</u> outline because we don't know the details of the project on which you are bidding. After you absorb the elements and reasoning behind this outline, however, we suggest you convert your outline to a <u>topical</u> outline, making your subheads topical, very specifically dealing with the project. If you do this:

- You establish the "theme" of the proposal.

- You discover the proposal has a message.

- You learn that writing to the outline becomes easier.

- You can predict the contents of a section or subsection.

Some proposal experts like a long Introduction, with your organization's capabilities introduced early to establish your credibility. Others suggest placing a brief Summary immediately following the Introduction.

Any outline that works for you is a good one. Use the following outline as you wish.

Cover Letter

The cover letter which transmits your proposal is an integral part of the message you want to convey. It should be written <u>last</u> because this is your <u>first</u> impact on the funding agency. Sound silly? Think about it. How can you write a cover letter until you know what you are transmitting.

In the section entitled "Detailed Suggestions on the Cover Letter and the Introduction" later in HOW TO WRITE A WINNING PROPOSAL, we discuss the contents of the cover letter in greater detail and give you a number of suggested first paragraphs for the letter, to get away from the boring, unimaginative, trite, over-used: "We are pleased to submit..."

Introduction

The Introduction is a brief review of your company's approach to the prospective customer's project. Perhaps the Introduction is only one page but it carries a strong sales message, stressing the unique approach you propose taking to work the project. We suggest you write this after the proposal has been written. to make sure all elements of the proposal are included.

The section referred to under the Cover Letter on the previous page also has some valuable tips on how to write a persuasive Introduction.

Statement of the Customer's Project

In this section, stress your understanding of the customer's project; but, by all means, don't just feed the customer's words back to him. This doesn't show that you understand the project...it only shows that you read the RFP.

It might be appropriate in this section, if you have such information, to describe the various approaches to solving the project which have been tried by others in the past. This would highlight your knowledge of the technical areas involved in this field.

Your Proposed Technical Approach to the Project

Describe the method by which you would attack the problem and describe the expected results. Bring out all that is new and innovative about your proposed technical approach. Emphasize your awareness of the value of the project to its field of application.

Your Organization's Capabilities and Past Experience

Describe the experience you have had in the past which qualifies you to perform on the proposed project. Describe in detail any internal Research and Development Programs your organization has conducted to enhance your capabilities in the field.

This section probably will include paragraphs which had been used in previous proposals and were pulled from the stored files. Particular care, therefore, must be taken to edit this copy to make it fit this particular proposal. Boiler plate that is obvious "boiler plate" can defeat your proposal. This subject is discussed in detail in the section on The Role of the Computer and Word Processor in Proposal Preparation.

If you have teaming agreements with other organizations, include information on their capabilities and show how these capabilities complement yours.

Include well-massaged resumes of the key persons who are being committed to the proposed project.

<u>And those resumes had better reflect
the specific experience called for
in the RFP</u>.

Project Management Plan

Describe the organization, structure, and schedule for managing the proposed project. Here you would insert the Work Breakdown Structure Chart or PERT Chart prepared by the cognizant Section Captain's team.

Stress the tight controls that will be exercised to ensure performance in a timely, cost-effective manner to guarantee on-time completion.

<u>Remember, Federal Government contracts now
are primarily fixed fee contracts.
If a contractor has a cost overrun,
the contractor has to eat it</u>.

It will be important to incorporate into this section, a detailed description of your Quality Control (Product Assurance) procedures. In a proposal for hardware, for example, you also need to stress the ways in which you have insured that parts will interface and interchange with other parts, and emphasize your plans for Configuration Control.

Pricing Criteria

As described in the job description for the Proposal Pricer, this information is presented as a separate and confidential section. Several elements are included in the price structure:

- **Direct Costs.** The details of salaries and wages are specified.

- **Operational Expenses.** The costs of doing business are given. As stated earlier, the prospective customer often provides a form to use in listing this information.

- **Indirect Costs.** The cost of managing the contract is given in detail. These costs include overhead and other standard costs and are usually shown in a lump sum. But don't forget: these costs must be substantiated in the proposal to insure credibility.

The Deliverables

The customer wants to know what he will receive in exchange for his money. The RFP will specify the "Deliverables" and your proposal must present a detailed plan for providing them.

Again, don't merely feed back the RFP's words. This can be fatal to your proposal.

It is necessary that you establish a definite schedule of progress reports and plan for their submission on a regular basis as specified in the RFP (i.e., monthly, quarterly, etc.). These reports are among the deliverables called out as an RFP requirement when the RFP refers to the Contract Data Requirements List (CDRL) items.

The detailed information on deliverables included in the proposal is as valuable to your organization as it is to the customer. The deliverables listing can help eliminate future problems and misunderstandings, and possible recriminations later on, if the project runs into any snags.

There are times when a contractor seems negligent and is blamed for over-running costs, and other "poor management" problems. It is possible that some of these seeming contractor shortcomings may have occurred because the customer found it necessary to change the scope of the contract and the contractor wasn't savvy enough to make sure these changes were properly and fully documented.

Keeping open the channels of communication, therefore, and making use of the reporting schedule for frequent one-on-one discussions, can keep many misunderstandings from developing:

- Both parties can use the reports to correct a program in mid-stream so its end results more closely meet its goals.

- The reports can show whether or not a program is successful in meeting its objectives.

- Properly documented deliverables can be the instrument by which both the customer and your organization can turn a faltering program into a successful program.

The Reality

There are four milestones in any proposal effort that must be passed before much can happen beyond them: (1) design freeze, so that what is being proposed cannot continue to change, (2) first draft assembled so a sounding can be done to see what remains, (3) pricing completed in sufficient time to permit sufficient review, and (4) final draft cutoff to permit the realtime needed for publication.

The schedule chart shown on page 31 (which looks backwards and really is) shows that to assign real dates to these events, pace backwards from the due date, allowing one day for packaging and bookcheck, added to whatever time is needed for delivery. Allow adequate time for printing and final production. Then make preliminary assignments, again by pacing backwards. Skip weekends and holidays (the team may have to work these days, but don't schedule them.)

Proposal contributors tend to ignore schedules if they haven't been consulted in advance and don't know they are critical and real, or if they are too complex. Like the man says: KISS (Keep it Simple, Stupid.)

SUGGESTED PROPOSAL PLAN

Write a Proposal Plan for presentation at the Proposal Kickoff Meeting. This clues everyone in and focuses their attention on the same goals and strategy. Some of the items to be included in a Proposal Plan are:

- Description of the project and your organization's approach and strategy in addressing the problem.

- Task descriptions.

- Team directory, with internal office extensions and home phone numbers.

- Format Instructions and Style Guide for Word Processors.

- WBS or PERT Chart, if prepared at this time.

- Designation of Personnel Available to Work the Project if given the award.

- Project Management Plan, including Quality Control Procedures.

- Proposal Schedule.

- Proposal Outline.

- Deliverable Items.

- The Customer's Evaluation Criteria.

Various elements contribute to the success of the Proposal Team and various devices need to be established to allow for coordination of information.

	1	2	3	4	5	S	S	6	7	8	9	10	S	S	11	12	13	14	15	S	S	16	17	18	19	20	S	S	21
DELIVER PROPOSAL																													▲
TO REPRODUCTION																									▲				
FINAL DRAFT APPROVED																							▲						
PRICING																		▲					▲						
FIRST DRAFT COMPLETE										▲																			
DESIGN FREEZE				▲																									

SUGGESTED AGENDA FOR PROPOSAL KICKOFF MEETING

The Proposal Kickoff Meeting is a good device for generating the team spirit discussed earlier. Various methods need to be used to allow for coordination of information. Brief proposal status meetings should be held periodically to make sure everyone is on schedule.

At the Proposal Kickoff Meeting:

- Present the Proposal Plan and discuss each item in detail.

- Define team members' assignments and deadlines.

- Describe proposal strategy and technical approach.

- Present Management approach, give input assignments and deadlines.

- Ask for resumes you don't have.

- Stress Industrial Security.

- Describe pricing approach and strategy, without giving figures.

- Discuss importance to adhering to proposal schedule.

OUR FAMOUS "ROAD MAP" IDEA

The first function of the Proposal Manager is to analyze the RFP. Sometimes, the writer of the RFP has already prepared an outline of the RFP - a "Road Map", if you will.

If such an outline is not already in the RFP, we suggest that the Proposal Manager's analysis be turned into a Road Map, for use first by the proposal team members and later by the customer's proposal evaluators.

This idea has worked "like magic" for previous users. Perhaps it will work its magic for you.

<u>It is known that a decision-maker seldom has time enough to read any part of the proposal except the Introduction which is inserted up front, and then this top person listens to the evaluators. And rightly so.</u>

The front matter, then, must be so dynamic that each evaluator and decision-maker really gets your message. Of primary importance is this:

<u>PLEASE</u>

<u>make sure your name or company logo
is printed at the top
of each sheet of paper
in the proposal.</u>

<u>Contracts have been lost
because an evaluator saw a good idea,
but couldn't remember whose good idea it was
because no company ID accompanied it.</u>

Then, prepare a <u>Road Map</u> for the evaluators. The prospective customer has taken great pains to spell out the requirements in the RFP, or in conversations, and when your proposal is submitted, the question is: Have you responded to each requirement? It is important to give the prospective customer everything listed as a requirement, but give them no more than they ask for.

As part of your pre-planning, you analyze the customer's requirements and prepare a form that serves several purposes during the preparation phase.

You may wish to start out with a form that takes very little adaptation to become the final insert for your proposal.

The left side of the form lists all requirements by paragraph number, page number, and RFP section, and gives a brief notation of the subject of the requirement.

On the right side of the form, you allow space to insert the paragraph number, page number, and section of the proposal where the response will appear. In addition, you have a column where the name of the individual who has responsibility for preparing the paragraph will appear. Therefore, you have built-in accountability, and this is important.

The form shown here might meet your needs.

RFP CHECKLIST

RFP REQUIREMENT				YOUR RESPONSE			
Para	Page	Section	Subject	Para	Page	Section	Responsibility

Or, you may find that a form similar to the one shown below is a handier tool for you to use in keeping track of your assigned proposal writers in accordance with the proposal schedule.

RFP Requirement	RFP Page	Your Proposal Response Page	Input Assigned To	Input Due Date	Input Delivered

The Road Map insures complete data for the evaluators. You insert the Road Map <u>immediately</u> following the Table of Contents in your finished proposal.

To review the sequence: Your Cover Letter tops the proposal. In the proposal proper you then give a detailed Table of Contents (and, if appropriate, a List of Illustrations and a List of Tables). Then you present the Road Map for the evaluators and the decision-maker. Your proposal's Introduction follows the Road Map.

The person who makes the final decision has it all laid out in a relatively brief form, and this could pay off with a contract award, and a QUICK one. It has happened.

PROPOSAL EVALUATION CRITERIA

In a number of places, we've referred to the customer's "Proposal Evaluators" and you might be saying: "Why all this fuss about making it easy for the evaluators to make their way through our proposal? We know we've met all the requirements."

You may know you've met their requirements, but it's important to let them know you have done so. Some RFP's give only general evaluation criteria. In other, more complex RFP's, greater detail is given about those standards on which the evaluation will be based - what requirements are in front of the evaluators as they read your proposal.

In most cases, the proposed cost is weighted heavily, presuming that all other requirements are met. The lowest bidder, with credibility, will receive the contract award.

In complex jobs, evaluation criteria can be listed in exquisite detail. Following is an example of the the evaluation points that could be given for a complex proposal covering an electronic equipment project.

580 Possible Points

200	Lowest cost proposal.
10	Lowest cost for each of 8 electronic work stations. Maximum possible score is 80.
10	Lowest cost for each of 5 supervisory electronic work stations. Maximum possible score is 50.
4	Lowest cost for each of 4 hard copy devices. Maximum possible score is 16.
2	Lowest cost for each of 7 CRT displays. Maximum possible score is 14.
10	Lowest cost for maintenance support. Maximum possible score is 10.
80	Technical Approach – Completeness, detail, and state-of-the-art status. Maximum possible score is 80.
60	Proposer's Related Experience – Costs, performance, schedules, and references given when previous customers are queried. Maximum possible score is 60.
60	Management Plan – Timeliness of schedule, quality and qualifications of personnel who are committed to work on the project if contact awarded. Maximum possible score is 60.
10	Location – Proximity of proposer's working location to main working location of prospective customer. Maximum possible score is 10.

Evaluation Factors	Maximum Possible Score
• Cost of System	370
• Proposed Technical Approach	80
• Related Experience	60
• Management Plan	60
• Proximity to Customer	10
TOTAL POINTS TO BE EARNED	580

AWARD WILL BE TO CONTRACTOR RECEIVING HIGHEST SCORE

THE ROLE OF THE COMPUTER AND WORD PROCESSOR IN PROPOSAL PREPARATION

Contributed by Charles W. Koch, Ph.D.

Over the last 10 years computers have profoundly changed the mechanics of writing. In 1976, authors typically used pencil and paper or, if they knew how, maybe they used a typewriter. This material then went through several proof-edit-retype cycles.

Today, word processing has replaced both typewriters and pencil and paper; word processing is the single most useful (and potentially most dangerous) computer application for proposal preparation. This is more than just a change in the mechanics of proposal preparation.

Definition of Word Processing

Maybe a definition of "word processing" is in order first. A "Word Processor" is a computer typewriter. As you type, keystrokes are recorded on a magnetic disk for later editing and/or printing.

All word processors show what you type as you type it. Some do this on a sheet of paper; most employ a video screen (called "CRT" for Cathode Ray Tube or "VDT" for Video Display Tube). For serious writing and editing, most companies use a word processor with a video screen.

Advantages of Word Processing

Even inexpensive word processing systems simplify the process of writing, editing and proofing. Here are some of the advantages:

- <u>Ease of Writing and Editing</u>. It is <u>much</u> easier to write and edit with a word processor than with any other writing implement, including pencil and paper. Words, paragraphs, and whole sections can be moved around, search capabilities make it easy to find text for editing or reference, and text can be inserted or deleted.

To take full advantage of the editing capabilities of word processing, the author must know how to type and be able to think with a keyboard instead of pencil and paper; this ability to think with a keyboard comes with practice. If the author must first write in longhand for later transcription by a typist, some of the advantages of word processing are lost.

- <u>Speedy Revision Cycles</u>. Since only changes are re-keyed between revision cycles, the time between revision cycles is shortened.

- **Less Chance of Introducing New Errors When Old Errors are Corrected.** With a typewriter, correcting an error often means retyping a page, which provides the danger of creating new errors. In word processing, only the error itself is corrected, eliminating the chance of introducing new errors.

- **Computerized Check of Spelling.** Most word processing systems come with programs for checking spelling. These spell checkers will catch 90 percent of your spelling errors, but they do have limitations.

  For example, if you come up with a typographical error that inadvertantly results in a legitimate word you didn't intend using — such as "from" being changed to "form" by your typo — the spell checker won't catch this error. And the spell checker doesn't recognize names or special jargon and so cannot check the spelling of those words.

  So you still have to proof the proposal, but now you can concentrate on proofing for content, and consistency, and grammar rather than on spelling errors.

- **More Time for the Intellectual Part of the Proposal Effort.** Since revisions can come fast and easy, less time need be spent on the mechanics of typing and proofing, and more can be spent honing the proposal content.

- **Late Revisions Are Possible.** Without a word processing system, the proposal writing and editing effort must cease well in advance of the delivery deadline, to give time for final typing and proofing.

- **Final Proofing is Easier.** With a word processing system, final proofing is more perfunctory (proofing should have been done for each revision), and final typing amounts to queuing the latest version to the computer printer.

> Don't forget, however, that you will still have to paste-up any needed illustrations and that the final product must be reproduced.

Pitfalls of Word Processing

Unfortunately, word processing can also be an invitation to intellectual laziness and sloppiness. Let's see how this can be so:

It is obviously a good idea to keep copies of old proposals and to re-use this material to create new ones. So far so good.

A seemingly minor improvement on this idea is to create a library of pre-approved descriptions of your company and its capabilities, project management write-ups, standard product descriptions, personnel resumes, and other sections common to most proposals. This type of pre-approved information is often called "boiler plate" material.

You could then create a new proposal by combining these general sections with new writeups (a process referred to as "massaging" or "slanting"), concentrating on the unique requirements of the project defined in the RFP.

<u>In fact, maybe you could do most of your proposals in their entirety from boiler plate</u>.

Disadvantages of "Boiler Plate"

Boiler plating, however, is possibly a <u>bad</u> idea. It can give a false sense of security which often leads the proposal team to ignore portions of the RFP, on the mistaken assumption that a particular requirement is already covered adequately in the standard boiler plate.

Boiler plating can also yield a final submission which looks just like what it is: a disjointed series of sections full of irrelevant detail, rather than a unified document aimed precisely at persuading the prospective customer that your company is uniquely qualified to do their work.

> Remember, if you are required to write a proposal to
> sell your ideas, your customer must believe that his
> needs are unique; otherwise, he would simply ask for
> a quote and issue a purchase order.

It is obviously bad politics to give your customer the impression that his needs are not really unique. A standardized proposal may convey that feeling - and you may as well just send him a brochure.

Emphasis Must Be Placed on Editing

Don't misunderstand. Please <u>do</u> copy sentences, paragraphs, even whole sections, from one proposal to another. Writing is tedious business, and the fastest, most elegant, and least error-prone way to do it is by copying <u>and editing</u>.

But keep the emphasis on the <u>editing</u> of copied material. The editing normally should be very heavy. <u>This</u> customer's RFP must be the guide for <u>this</u> proposal. Even if the identical item or service was required earlier by another customer, it will not be sufficient to merely change the cover letter and reprint the old proposal for the new customer.

Instead, go through the intellectual effort of rewriting the proposal: that is, analyze the RFP, decide what should be emphasized and what should merely be mentioned, prepare an outline, create a project team, assign writing responsibilities, and so forth.

Then, by all means, use the old material; but be sure it is re-organized, edited, padded, and excised of irrelevant and/or unasked-for information.

In other words, the old material should be used to cure writers' cramp, not used as a substitute for the intellectual effort of examining the customer's specific requirements and responding to them, specifically.

COMPUTER PRINTERS

OR

TO TYPESET OR NOT TO TYPESET

Before you begin to write the proposal, decide how the final copy is going to look. The most basic decision is whether the final copy is to be type<u>script</u> or type<u>set</u>.

"Type<u>script</u>" refers to typewriter-looking text;

"Type<u>set</u>" refers to text which looks like the higher-quality print in books or magazines.

Here is a list of the merits and demerits of each option:

<u>Merits</u>	<u>Demerits</u>
Type<u>script</u>:	
-Inexpensive	-Less professional look
-Fast to produce	-Less legible
-Doesn't look "frivolous" or "over-produced"	-Fewer words per page
	-Limited type styles:
	-Heads and subheads get lost
	-More difficult to emphasize text
	-Two-column format not recommended
Type<u>set</u>:	
-More professional look	-But may seem 'overdone'
-More legible	-More expensive and time consuming
-Wide variety of type sizes and styles can be used to show <u>structure</u> of the proposal, and to <u>emphasize</u> points	
-More compact – important for page-limited projects	
-Two-column format can be used to achieve even more compaction and greater legibility	

Let's discuss only a few of the issues mentioned in the table:

- Legibility. Numerous experiments have shown beyond doubt that people read typeset copy faster - and retain what they have read longer - than when they have to read comparable typescript copy. There are many reasons:

    - Proportional Spacing. In typeset copy, the letter spacing for an "m", for example, is greater than for an "n". This makes it easy to distinguish the letters. Most typescript copy uses unit spacing in which all letters, regardless of actual width, occupy the same amount of space, thus making it more difficult for the reader to distinguish different letters.

    - More Words Per Line. The proportional spacing of typeset copy yields more words per line because narrow letters such as "l", "i", and "t" are more common than wide letters such as "m" and "w"; and because lower-case letters, which occupy less line space, are more common than upper case letters, which occupy more line space (compare the "l" and the "L", for example.)

    - Unit space type (that is, typescript style) must be designed so the largest, most complex letters fit into the space provided. This means that narrow letters squander line space, and that typescript copy is very "loose". In other words, the eye has to travel more to take in the same number of words.

    - Superior Emphasis. With typeset copy, the wide variety of type sizes and styles makes it possible to emphasize both the structure of the document and particularly important points, without interfering with legibility.

    - Heads Stand Out. Typically, the structure of a typescript document is shown by printing heads in a larger and heavier type than that of the text. In a typeset document emphasis can be achieved by using italics or slanted type in the text.

- **Fewer Options Are Available For Typescript Documents.** In most cases, variation in type style is limited to using upper case letters or underscoring. However, both upper case text and underscored text is more difficult to read than normal text.

- **Typescript Decreases Legibility.** Hence, for typescript documents, use of variable indents or margin settings is often used to show the structure of the document. However, this has the undesirable side effect of decreasing the number of words per line which, in turn, decreases legibility. Changes in margin settings are less called for, and are less common, in typeset documents.

- **Compactness.** Typeset copy is more compact than typescript copy because of the proportional-space and superior-emphasis features just described. Compactness can be a critical issue on its own merits if the RFP limits you to a certain number of pages.

- **Two-Column Format.** Assuming that your proposal will be submitted on standard 8-1/2 x 11 inch paper, a two column format, combined with typesetting, has much to recommend it:

  - **Legibility Is Enhanced** When eye-travel between right and left margins is diminished, as is the case with the two-column format, legibility is enhanced.

  - **More Words Per Page.** A two-column format usually puts more words on a page than does a single-column format. At first this sounds surprising because space seems "lost" in the "gutter" (white space) between columns. But the lost space is more than made up for by these next three factors:

  - **Less Space is Squandered By "Widows".** - "Widows" is the term given the unused portion of a line following the end of a paragraph or of a head.

  - **Single-Column Illustrations and Tables Can be Used.** - This can save considerable space.

- **Omits Extra Space Between Paragraphs.** – In single-column formats, it is traditional to add some extra white space, or "leading", between paragraphs to enhance legibility. This is not needed in two-column formats.

- **The Two-Column Format Is Well Worth the Effort.** The two-column format, on 8-1/2 by 11 inch paper, gives a more professional appearance to the document. The Two-Column format is occasionally used with type_script_ documents for some of the reasons listed above. but this format seems to combine best with type_set_ documents.

SUMMARY OF THE COMPUTER DISCUSSION

In summary, storing the related experience of your organization in the computer for easy recall, saves the humongous amount of personnel hours formerly used for manual storage in file cabinets.

In addition, use of word processing gives you more time for the intellectual part of the proposal effort and helps you produce a superior proposal because word processing will:

- Make it easier to re-use and massage material from earlier projects.

- Reduce the time required to cycle revisions.

- Prevent the introduction of mechanical errors during retyping.

- Automate proofing for spelling errors

In short, word processing relieves much of the drudgery of writing. When combined with the appropriate printer or typesetter, word processing can also improve the "look" of your final document.

A "STORYBOARD" APPROACH TO PROPOSAL PREPARATION

In the early 1960's, the aerospace industry followed the lead of the motion picture studios and began using the "Storyboard Approach" to proposal preparation - the technique of "writing on the walls."

Strictly speaking, the original storyboard format for proposals included two 2-column facing pages which dealt with one topic. When you turned the page, you changed the topic.

Proposal Managers who have tried marshalling the proposal team to write the proposal using the adaptation of the storyboard approach, as suggested in HOW TO WRITE A WINNING PROPOSAL, have said: "It may seem like an expensive approach, but it sure pays off."

What to YOU want?
A cheap way to write a proposal?
Or do you want a Contract?

The storyboard technique is valuable where a team of individuals is writing a proposal.

Storyboarding is a group writing process that helps achieve clarity, cross-fertilization of ideas, coherence, and tight control. This method is a means of continuing a "brain storming" process from the planning stage through to proposal delivery. Modified to meet your needs - even if your proposal is a small, one-person effort - writing on the walls might be an answer for you.

The illustration here reveals how the work goes when preparing a proposal the conventional way, with each person writing alone at a desk, not knowing what others are writing, duplicating text, taking different approaches, feeling confused, and splattered in all directions.

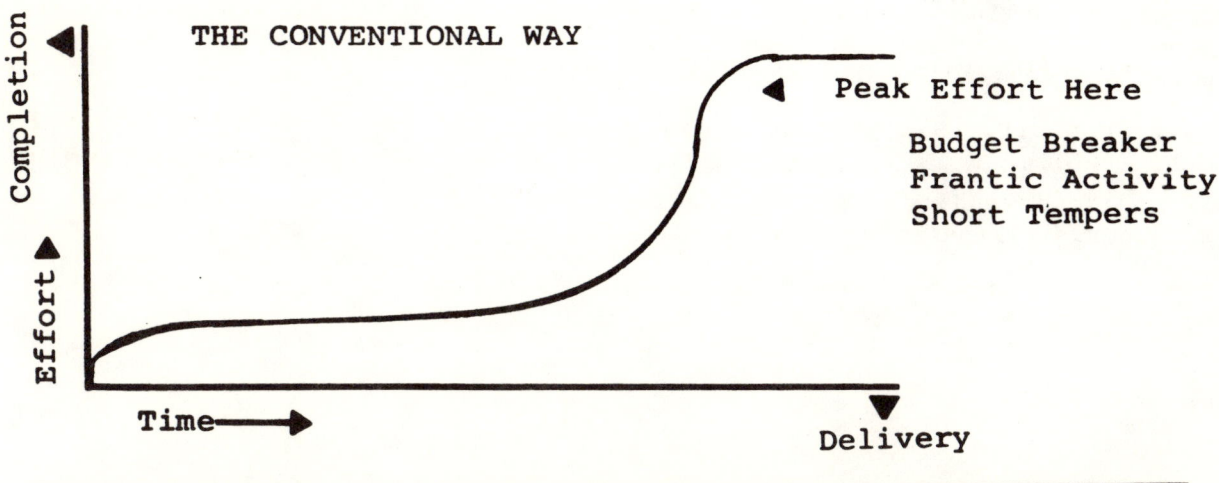

Here is how the effort peaks early when the proposal is written the "Storyboard" way:

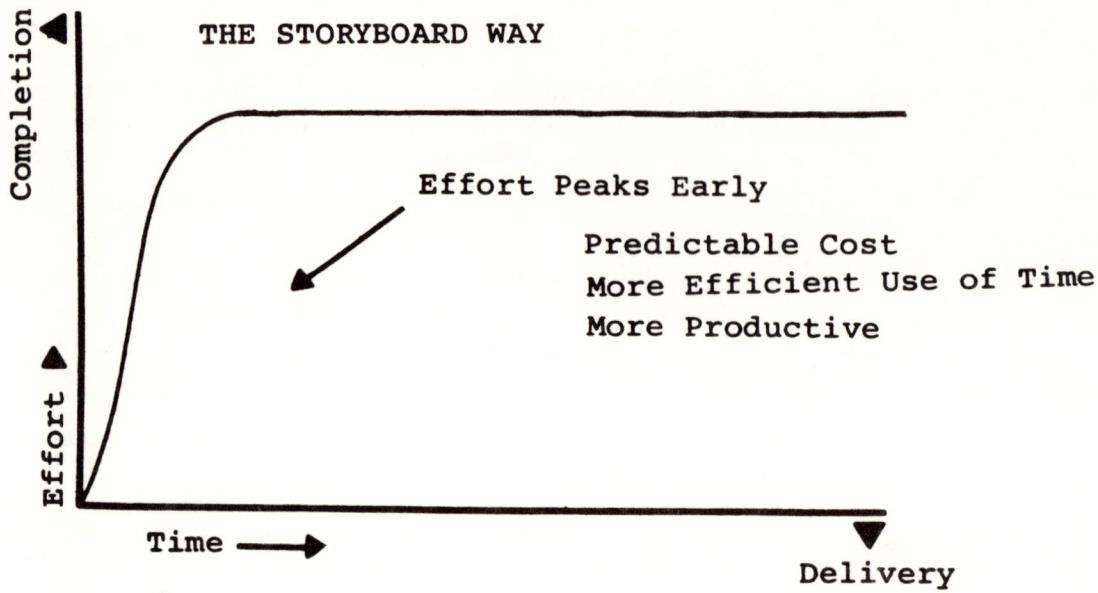

THE STORYBOARD WAY

Effort Peaks Early
Predictable Cost
More Efficient Use of Time
More Productive

This is how you would proceed: Designate a room with plenty of wall space. The written pages can be pinned to the wall with push pins if the walls are dry wall or Celotex. As an alternative, large sheets of brown paper can be taped to the wall with masking tape, and the pages taped to the brown paper.

With a heavy black or red ink marker, write the headings from your detailed outline on pieces of paper large enough to be seen across the room. By this time, you have "sized" the proposal and know how many pages are desired in each section.

Pin the headings on the wall and under each heading (5 across) pin blank sheets of paper to reserve the space for the writer of that section. (This tends to control the inputter whose topic is important enough to deserve <u>six</u> pages of copy but not the <u>20</u> he comes in with.)

As the section is written and printed in rough, pin the paper on the wall in their reserved spaces, removing the blank sheets. Rough graphics are pinned to the wall where desired.

Soon, your proposal begins to take shape on the wall. It becomes immediately apparent who is meeting the deadline - and who is not. "Danger" signs can be placed where input is lagging and adversely affecting the possibility of on-time delivery.

All members of the team should read all portions of the proposal as it is growing. This can eliminate duplication and can show the way to plug holes that need filling.

The Proposal Manager can review the proposal constantly, and can suggest rewrites to eliminate unnecessary redundancy, strengthen the message, and develop cohesion and singleness of approach.

THE MANAGEMENT REVIEW PROCESS

The first fruits of a collaborative effort are nearly always flawed; the purpose of the review is to find out what's wrong with the proposal as a product - what's missing or awry - and to fix it. Those who are writing the proposal are so intimately involved with it that their views are necessarily subjective. Members of the review committee are persons who can be objective in their evaluation. They are insurance that no major error has occurred.

Proposal review covers the entire cycle of critical reading, rewriting, and editing, beginning with the reviewer's evaluation of the initial outline. The purpose of the review is to insure that the goals basic to every proposal are met; to:

- Present an adequate and economical technical solution to the customer's problem as defined in the RFP.

- Respond to the RFP point-by-point.

- Frame a business deal that is attractive to the customer; one that has been specifically approved by your company's responsible management.

- Assure the customer that the project will be completed as promised - on time, to specifications, within cost.

- Advocate your company's cause - persuasively.

The Proposal Manager and top management should review the proposal to insure that it meets the funding agency requirements, truthfully reflects your capabilities, standards, and goals, and carries a strong sales message. The proposal must be reviewed early and continually in the preparation cycle to influence its shape and tone.

When reviewing the proposal:

- Look for unbalanced emphasis between topics.

- Watch for the hesitant writer who turns in two pages when you wanted six pages on the topic. His blank sheets left on the wall will help you make your point.

- Watch for that eager writer referred to earlier, who gives you 20 pages when you wanted six.

Also look out for.

- Conflicting sales messages.
- Weak sales message or no sales message at all.
- Over-repetition.
- Stating a case and failing to prove it.
- Furnishing proof before stating a case.
- Lack of graphics.
- Over-Complex graphics.
- Graphics that don't apply.
- And, above all - Does the proposal "play"?

STORYBOARD REVIEWING WALL

SPECIAL NOTE TO MANAGEMENT REVIEWERS

Perhaps the most important point to remember in this matter of Management Review is this: Reviewers must present a consistent approach to the inputters.

A painful case witnessed occurred when a technical management reviewer and an administrative management reviewer strongly disagreed on changes needed to bring a section of written copy to their requirements. This situation became so disagreeable that the writer was shaken and unable to produce an acceptable rewrite. Sound extreme? Blame the writer? Don't. This can happen, and it can be disastrous.

SPECIAL NOTE TO INPUTTERS

Reviewers make their comments in writing, and authors should review each comment; evaluate its appropriateness to the overall write-up and to the overall proposal theme and strategy. It must be considered that reviewers have the broader vision of how this particular write-up fits into the whole and may have other inputs of which you could not be aware.

It is acknowledged that the author might have strong feelings as to how the write-up was written originally and may wish to discuss the suggested changes with the reviewers. The author then probably rewrites the copy to reflect at least some of the reviewer comments.

Let's face it: there are times when it is good politics to integrate management suggestions into the copy.

At any rate, make sure reviewers receive feedback from the inputters whose copy they reviewed.

DETAILED SUGGESTIONS ON THE COVER LETTER
AND
THE INTRODUCTION

AN ATTENTION-GRABBING COVER LETTER

Present your understanding of the overall program or problem. Assert your qualifications for the job. State that your sweet words are backed with hard commitments of personnel, machines, facilities, and capabilities - in other words, true expertise. Spell out top management's interest, enthusiasm, and backing. Hammer home the basic themes of the proposal. Show the advantages of a sound and sane business deal.

The main thought in the reader's mind is: "What's in it for me?" Answer that question and you'll have an avid reader. He is, remember, intensely interested in the subject to begin with.

Make your cover letter a summation of the proposal, not a presentation of every major facet of the design. Be specific and forward in your assertions: "Our approach is unique..."We have developed this before"..."We speak with confidence"..."We are experienced"..."Our costs are lower than we anticipated..."

You want to give the impression, you know, that this is a competent company talking, not two guys operating out of a telephone booth.

In your summation, along with turning the spotlight on your company, place your major sales points up front, where they can be seen.

Keep the sales point relevant to the subject: study projects depend on qualified team members (and cost), development programs depend on experience and facilities (and cost), software development programs depend on expertise, management know-how, and facilities (and cost). The cover letter should discuss appropriate themes. Credibility gaps occur when a proposer claims he can solve the world's problems in a six-month study.

Very few customers really buy puffery and they recognize it, so be leary of it; the description of the job to be done must match up with the overall costs, or credibility goes out the window.

Direct the letter toward the decision-making level of the customer's organization, no matter how many levels of readership you know are involved.

An old saying to keep in mind: "Never over-estimate your audience's knowledge, never under-estimate its intelligence." Writing the cover letter is a tough writing job, so consider finding and using the best writer in the company. The end result will be a better letter.

Now that you've covered all the points made above, you ask: How long should a cover letter be?

The answer is: <u>one page, of course</u>. (Well, what else did you expect?)

NINE "SELLING" OPENINGS FOR COVER LETTERS

1. The Blank Company appreciates the opportunity to submit this proposal, which is fully responsive in all respects to your Request for Proposal No. 123456. A "Road Map" to assist Evaluators in finding our response to each requirement called out in the RFP can be found immediately following the Table of Contents.

2. We in the Blank Company are particularly proud to be associated with the "Z" Program. This is the type of program toward which we have directed our long-range plans for the Blank Company and the "Z" Program allows us to apply the technical skill we have built over the years and to focus on objectives of immediate benefit to your Agency. A "Road Map" to assist Evaluators in finding our response to each of your requirements called out in the RFP can be found immediately following the Table of Contents.

3. The Blank Company proposes to do the systems analysis in support of the "Z" Program. We have followed the "Z" concept closely and are familiar with the technical and program details to date. A "Road Map" to assist Evaluators in finding our response to each of your requirements called out in the RFP can be found immediately following the Table of Contents.

Cover Letter "Selling" Openings (Cont'd.)

4   The Blank Company submits for your consideration this proposal for the formulation and evaluation of integrated "Z" concepts. These concepts will integrate and optimize the joint usage of "Z's" in conjunction with the many types of other "Z's" now operational or planned. A "Road Map" to assist Evaluators in finding our response to each of your requirements called out in the RFP can be found immediately following the Table of Contents.

5.   As a result of recent discussions with Mr. Thomas Atkinson, Project Manager for your company, the Blank Company is submitting this unsolicited proposal.

      This proposal suggests that our Mr. Peter Andrews, an acknowledged expert in his field, undertake the six-month study Mr. Atkinson told us your company requires to statistically determine the deleterious human factors which may be present in the sound waves in a modern boiler factory.

6   The Blank Company welcomes this opportunity for further participation in the Navy's effort to increase the Fleet to the number of ships desired by the Chief of Naval Operations (CNO). This proposal presents the culmination of two years of preparation by our company for this procurement.

      In anticipation of the Navy's need for competent contractor assistance in this program, the Blank Company engaged in intensive internal Research and Development Programs in sonar countermeasures, which are within our particular area of expertise.

      We are especially pleased to report that, as a result, the Blank Company has developed certain electronic devices that enhance a ship's listening capability.

Cover Letter "Selling" Openings (Cont'd.)

7. The Blank Company proposes to assist your Agency in performing analyzes in general support of the "Z" Program. The analyses proposed will point the way toward feasible alternatives for improving performance and reducing life cycle costs. Data produced under this project can be used in making decisions so necessary in bringing to full fruition a program with the system implications of "Z".

8. This proposal represents the culmination of nearly three years of preparation for this procurement by the Blank Company. During this period, we have developed innovative state-of-the-art concepts in hardware and software, designed to place our products far ahead of others in our field of expertise.

9. The Blank Company's demonstrated leadership and acknowledged superiority in software and hardware systems support is the basis for this proposal to install a system that will do the job described as a requirement in the Statement of Work (SOW) included in RFP No. 123456. Because of our track record in this field, we believe we are uniquely qualified to meet your needs.

<u>It is no use to wait
for your ship to come in
unless you have sent one out.</u>

Writing A Persuasive Introduction

A good Introduction summarizes in specific terms the main selling points of the proposal; gives the significant reasons why your company should win the contract. The Introduction is a key opportunity to give the customer a clear picture of what the real persuaders are.

When you write the Introduction, try to put yourself in the customer's place and answer this question: "What's in it for me?" Why is your technical approach so good? Are there any ideas that are unique to your company that they could be highlighted? What are the strengths in your approach that you want to stress to the customer.

Perhaps the element to emphasize is the company's directly related experience and the fact that some of the key people in related technical areas will be performing the work or serving as high-level reviewers of the work done by the performers.

All this sounds very fundamental, but here are some examples of the usual Introduction.

- There's the one that starts by declaring that this proposal is in response to RFP XXX.XXX. This has already been said on the cover page and on the shipping invoice.

- Then there's the Introduction that summarizes the contents of the proposal without bringing out any significant points - just summarizes it. This also has been done earlier - by the Table of Contents.

- And then there's the Introduction that offers a two or three paragraph synopsis of the RFP requirements or the work statements. This proves only that someone at least read the RFP. This is not a selling point.

None of this is intended to imply that a well-written Introduction is going to sell the whole proposal; it only means the Introduction should bring out the main selling points.

You might try writing a first draft of the Introduction at the beginning of the proposal effort. Get something down on paper, no matter how bad it looks. Use it as a guide to help you concentrate on the big picture. Read it over frequently; change it as you go. By the end of the proposal preparation period, it will have helped you do a lot of basic thinking and you may even have a pretty good draft of your Introduction.

SOME POINTS TO REMEMBER

Now that the Proposal Manager's photograph has been ripped to shreds by darts, it's time to look back at what the team has accomplished.

As stated earlier, everything that could be written about how to write a winning proposal would fill a library, and only highlights, really, have been dealt with in HOW TO WRITE A WINNING PROPOSAL. Here are some points you surely remember:

- The purpose of the proposal was to "sell" you to your prospective customer.

- The Proposal Manager's job was to produce a clear, concise, selling, logical, cohesive document.

- An expert - but not fancy - document was essential. You didn't let a SCHLOCKY production technique detract from your message.

- You set up your proposal preparation deadlines and schedule and then you were a BEAR so you could deliver the proposal on time. (This was when your team welcomed the darts.) You were constantly aware that a late proposal is automatically disqualified. Since a proposal effort costs money, time, labor, and expenses (and sometimes blood, sweat, and tears), you didn't let your proposal go down the drain by missing the deadline.

- If your proposal is selected as the "winner" by the customer, the job isn't in the bag as it was submitted. "Winning" has just given you your place at the negotiating table where the fine points are honed until you and the customer are in final agreement.

For your information, this book was written on a WANG Word Processor and the original was printed in typescript on a WANG Laser Printer.

YOU CAN'T WIN 'EM ALL

Keep in mind - despite the title of this book - you can't win 'em all. Make the most of unsuccessful bids. If you didn't receive the award, ask the funding agency why. (Do this with an "I want to learn from this" attitude. Stay away from "poor little me.")

Hold a critique in your company with top management and all cognizant personnel present. Pass on to these people what the agency said about your proposal. You may see that you did inadequate marketing and advance planning. Perhaps your background and previous experience did not persuade the agency personnel that you could perform on the project alone and that your company should team with qualified partners in the future.

Keep any rejected proposal in your files, and keep what you learned from it on a "back burner" in your mind. Another project might come to your attention where your proposal will fit perfectly, with just a few revisions, and you may be able to turn a losing proposal into a winner.

Just don't give up. Perseverance can pay off.

"For a while there, I thought we'd never get the damn thing finished."

NOW, IS THIS THE END?

So, with the help of this book, you have written a proposal. It wasn't easy, but you succeeded in saying what you wanted to say. You delivered your proposal.

You think this is the end...that this was your last proposal?

AH, NO.   IT'S ONLY THE BEGINNING...

this month

Fairfax County Public Library   September 1989

From 1939 to Today. *In 50 years, Fairfax County Public Library has progressed from this tiny cinderblock building to a system of 22 branches and a collection of more than two million items.*

Numbers stack up at the library

Warning: Library use can be habit-forming. And if you're like most people in Fairfax County, you may already know the consequences.

Improved reading skills, a richer imagination and self-directed education are just some of the many benefits of this "habit."

In a county of 746,600 residents, the collection of 2.5 million titles spent more time in the hands of readers than on library shelves. The 8.5 million loans in fiscal year 1989 equalled 11 items for each man, woman and child in the county.

The 8.5 million circulation figure represents a three percent increase over the 1988 total. For most public libraries serving comparable populations (500,000 to 999,999 people) circulation is closer to 3 million items, according to the American Library Association.

About 370,000 items were added to the library's collection.

Fourteen branches reported gains in circulation this year, including the Fair Oaks Mini Library. From its convenient location in the Fair Oaks Mall, that branch recorded more than 116,000 loans, making it the busiest of seven mini-branches.

The total gain in circulation could mean that Fairfax County Public Library will again be named the busiest library system in the South. This past spring the annual Memphis/Shelby County survey designated the library as the "most active" of 94 systems in 15 southern U.S. states.

More than 167,800 people attended the library's 4,300 programs, including the Summer Reading Game for school-age children. The same number of people would fill Capital Center for nine sold-out performances. The Arena Stage theater would be SRO for 203 nights, and if you didn't have a ticket to the Barns at Wolf Trap, you'd have to wait a year and 114 nights for a seat.

That's a lot of people, however you figure it.

Program highlights

■ Walk like an Egyptian: Henry Kramer, Egyptologist, offers travel tips on Sept. 11, at 7:30, Dolley Madison Library.

■ John Hickman, WAMU broadcaster, discusses vintage radio, programs and stars, at Patrick Henry Library on Sept. 21 at 7:30.

■ John Marshall Library's annual Pet Show, open to all kinds of pets, is Sept. 23 from 1-2:30. Registration begins at 12:45. Judges this year include Joseph Gartlan, State Senator 36th District; Gladys Keating, delegate to the Virginia Assembly, and other dignitaries, with awards in 14 categories.

■ If you're concerned about eating better food, with less fat and cholesterol, the American Heart Association's Culinary Hearts Kitchen series is for you. The six-week series explains how to select and prepare tasty, nutritious food. A healthier lifestyle begins at Pohick Regional Library on Sept. 25, at 7:30.

■ Author Richard Galloway discusses "The Common Soldier in the American Civil War" on Sept. 5, 7:30, Sherwood Regional Library.

■ Richard Byrd Library hosts two lectures for getting a job with the County: with the public schools on Sept. 12 at 7:30, and with other agencies on Sept. 20 at 7:30.

Inside...

☐ **Library news**

☐ **September schedule for adult and children's programs**

☐ **Literary quiz**

Marginalia

Holiday closings: The library will be closed September 3 and 4 for Labor Day.

■ ■ ■ ■ ■ ■ ■ ■ ■ ■

Don't forget to register! All programs are free, but space is limited. All programs require registration, unless noted. To register, call or visit the library beginning two weeks before the event.

■ ■ ■ ■ ■ ■ ■ ■ ■ ■

The Library Board meets at Tysons-Pimmit Regional Library in Falls Church on Wednesday, Sept. 20, at 7:30. For more information, call 246-5209.

■ ■ ■ ■ ■ ■ ■ ■ ■ ■

Free plant clinics, sponsored by the Extension Service, are held each week at many library branches. For information, call 246-5393.

■ ■ ■ ■ ■ ■ ■ ■ ■ ■

Voter registration is available during all open hours at the six regional libraries, and from 7 p.m. on Wednesdays and Thursdays, and all day Saturdays, at most other branches. Call your neighborhood branch to confirm availability.

■ ■ ■ ■ ■ ■ ■ ■ ■ ■

Programs may be signed for the deaf. To schedule an interpreter, call 971-6612 (TDD or voice).

Program Guide

Programs require advance registration, unless noted.

BURKE CENTRE
5661 Burke Centre Parkway
Burke * 250-6400
M,TH 10-6; TU,W 1-9; SA 9-5; F,SU Closed

Tuesdays, Sept. 5 & 12, 7:00
Twilight Tales. Stories for age 3-5.

CENTREVILLE
14114B Lee Highway
Centreville * 830-2223
M,TH 1-9; TU,W 10-9; F 10-6; SA 9-5; SU Closed

Thursday, Sept. 14, 10:30
All About Me. Stories and activities. Age 2 with adult.

Fridays, Sept. 15 & 22, 11:00
When I Go to School. Stories and activities. Age 3-5 with adult.

Thursday, Sept. 21, 1:00
Digging for Dinosaurs. Stories and activities. Age 3-5.

Thursday, Sept. 21, 7:30
Face the SATs with Confidence. For students and parents, Fort Hill Bldg, 5900 Centreville Road, #205.

DOLLEY MADISON
1244 Oak Ridge Avenue
McLean * 356-0770
M,TH 1-9; TU,W 10-9; F 10-6; SA 9-5; SU Closed

Thursdays, Sept. 7-28, 2:30
50th Anniversary Classic Films. *My Man Godfrey, Abe Lincoln in Illinois, Boom Town, Swiss Miss.*

Monday, Sept. 11, 7:30
Egypt: Where it All Began. Travel lecture with Egyptologist Henry Kramer.

Wednesday, Sept. 13, 7:30
Face the SATs with Confidence. For students and parents.

Tuesday, Sept. 19, 7:00
Understanding Social Security and Medicare. Cosponsored by Financial Education Center.

FAIRFAX CITY
3915 Chain Bridge Rd.
Fairfax * 246-2281
M-TH 9-9; F 9-6; SA 9-5; SU 12-8

Tuesdays, Sept. 5-26, 9:30
Humpty Dumpty and Company. Nursery rhymes and stories. Age 2-3 with adult.

Tuesdays, Sept. 5-26, 7:15
Sleepytime Stories. Bedtime stories. Age 3-5 with adult. Wear pajamas, bring stuffed toy.

Mondays, Sept. 11-25, 9:30
Elephants and Friends. Stories, games about elephants, mice and other animals. Age 4-5.

Tuesdays, Sept. 12 & 19, 7:00
Complete Financial Planning. Mary Ginn.

Thursday, Sept. 14, 7:15
Proposal Writing. With Thomas Charland.

Saturday, Sept. 16, 2:00
Wednesday, Sept. 20, 7:00
Face the SATs with Confidence. For students and parents.

Monday, Sept. 18, 2:30
Billions of Bubbles. Take home bubble pipe. Age 5-8.

Tuesday, Sept. 26, 7:00
PC Software for Financial Planning. Coleman Bevis.

GEORGE MASON
7001 Little River Turnpike
Annandale * 256-3800
M-TH 9-9; F 9-6; SA 9-5; SU 12-8

Thursdays, Sept. 7-21, 1:30
A Family Affair. Stories, games, activities. Age 3-5.

Tuesday, Sept. 12, 7:30
Face the SATs with Confidence. For students and parents.

Wednesday, Sept. 13, 7:00
Retirement Planning for Government Employees. John Lynch, Financial Education Center.

Mondays, Sept. 18 & 25, 10 & 11
Two for Twos. Stories for age 2 with adult.

Friday, Sept. 22, 9-6:00
Saturday, Sept. 23, 9-5:00
Sunday, Sept. 24, noon-5:00
George Mason Book Sale. Sponsored by Friends of the Library.

Thursday, Sept. 28, 7:00
The Supreme Court and the Constitution: What Would the Founding Fathers Think?

HUNTERS WOODS
2355A Hunters Woods Plaza
Reston * 860-2602
M,TH 10-6; TU,W 1-9; SA 9-5; F,SU Closed

Saturday, Sept. 16, 11:00
Tuesday, Sept. 19, 2:00
Rain and Rainbows. Stories, craft and fingerplays. Age 3-5.

JOHN MARSHALL
6209 Rose Hill Drive
Alexandria * 971-0010
M,TH 1-9; TU,W 10-9; F 10-6; SA 9-5; SU Closed

Wednesdays, Sept. 13-27, 10:30
Time for Twos. Stories and activities. Age 2 with adult.

Wednesday, Sept. 13, 7:15
Publishing or Marketing Your Writing. Pat Hyland.

Thursdays, Sept. 14-28, 1:00, age 3 with adult; 2:00 age 4-5.
Bread and Butter Tales. Stories and activities.

Tuesday, Sept. 19, 7:00
Spreadsheet Design for Budgeting. David Rosenberg, Financial Education Center.

Saturday, Sept. 23, 1:00
Raindate, Sept. 30
John Marshall Library's Annual Pet Show. All pets welcome.

Friday, Sept. 29, 10:00
Goosey, Goosey, Gander. Nursery rhymes and songs. Age 12-23 months with adult.

50th anniversary special events

Thursdays, Sept. 7-28, 2:30
Classic Film Series. *My Man Godfrey, Boom Town,* and others.
Dolley Madison Library, McLean, 356-0770

Fairfax County Public Library
50th anniversary
"the past is prologue"

Wednesday, Sept. 13, 10-2:00
50th Anniversary Reception. Commemorative hand-made quilt on display. Reston Regional Library, Reston, 689-2700.

Banned Books Week
September 23-30

Freedom to Read

In 1989, the Ayatollah Khomeini encouraged his followers to "execute" the author of *The Satanic Verses,* because the book was offensive to Muslim teachings. Public response elevated it to the best-seller list, and developed a parallel interest in alternative readings of Muslim works.

Banned Books Week, September 23-30, celebrates the cross-cultural education process in books and reading.

AMERICAN HERITAGE DICTIONARY • THE BIBLE • ARE YOU THERE, GOD? IT'S ME, MARGARET • OUR BODIES, OURSELVES • TARZAN ALICE'S ADVENTURES IN WONDERLAND • THE EXORCIST • THE CHOCOLATE WAR • CATCH-22 • LORD OF THE FLIES • ORDINARY PEOPLE • SOUL ON ICE • RAISIN IN THE SUN • OLIVER TWIST • A FAREWELL TO ARMS • THE BEST SHORT STORIES OF NEGRO WRITERS • FLOWERS FOR ALGERNON • ULYSSES • TO KILL A MOCKINGBIRD • ROSEMARY'S BABY • THE FIXER • DEATH OF A SALESMAN • MOTHER GOOSE • CATCHER IN THE RYE • THE MERCHANT OF VENICE • ONE DAY IN THE LIFE OF IVAN DENISOVICH • GRAPES OF WRATH • THE ADVENTURES OF HUCKLEBERRY FINN • SLAUGHTERHOUSE-FIVE • GO ASK ALICE

Sponsored by the American Booksellers Association, American Library Association, American Society of Journalists and Authors, and other national groups, Banned Books Week carries a potent message. It calls attention to the freedoms we enjoy, freedom of speech and freedom of the press, and stresses the importance of making information, even unorthodox or unpopular viewpoints, readily available to all.

In defense of our inalienable rights, John F. Kennedy said, "We are not afraid to entrust the American people with unpleasant facts, foreign ideas, alien philosophies, and competitive values. For a nation that is afraid to let its people judge the truth and falsehood in an open market is a nation that is afraid of its people."

KINGS PARK
9000 Burke Lake Road
Burke * 978-5600
M,TH 1-9; TU,W 10-9; F 10-6; SA 9-5; SU 12-8

Tuesday, Sept. 5, 10:30
Wednesday, Sept. 6, 10:30
Friday, Sept. 8, 10:30
September Sampler for Ones. Stories, fingerplays, rhymes. Age 16-23 months with adult.

Tuesday, Sept. 5, 7:30
Book Discussion Group. *Tess of the D'Ubervilles,* by Thomas Hardy.

Thursday, Sept. 7, 7:30
Face the SATs with Confidence. For students and parents.

Monday, Sept. 18, 7:30
How to Develop a Grant Proposal. Sandy Matthews.

Tuesday, Sept. 19, 10:30
Wednesday, Sept. 20, 10:30
Friday, Sept. 22, 10:30
September Sampler for Twos. Stories, fingerplays, rhymes. Age 2 with adult.

Tuesday, Sept. 19, 2:00
Tuesday, Sept. 26, 10:30 & 1:30
September Sampler for Fours and Fives. Stories, rhymes, puppets. Age 4-5 with adult.

Wednesday, Sept. 20, 7:00
Banks and Banking Services. Rick Frank, Financial Education Center.

Thursday, Sept. 21, 1:30
Wednesday, Sept. 27, 10:30
Friday, Sept. 29, 10:30
September Sampler for Threes. Stories, fingerplays, rhymes. Age 3 with adult.

Sunday, Sept. 24, 2:00
Pancake Party. Stories and pancake treat. Age 3-5 with adult.

Wednesday, Sept. 27, 7:00
Home Equity Loans. Rick Frank, Financial Education Center.

MARTHA WASHINGTON
6614 Fort Hunt Road
Alexandria * 768-6700
M,TH 1-9; TU,W 10-9; F 10-6; SA 9-5; SU Closed

Tuesdays, Sept. 12-26, 10:30
Time for Twos. Stories and activities. Age 2 with adult.

Wednesdays, Sept. 13-27, 10:00, age 3 with adult; 11:00, age 4-5.
Bread and Butter Tales. Stories and activities.

Wednesday, Sept. 13, 10:00
Reverse Mortgages. Bronwyn Billings, Financial Education Center.

Friday, Sept. 15, 10:00
Goosey, Goosey, Gander. Nursery rhymes and songs. Age 12-23 months with adult.

CHANNEL 44 DAILY PROGRAM SCHEDULE
BEGINS SEPTEMBER 4

2:30-3:00 IN PRINT, a book talk show from Beverly Hills.

3:00-3:30 KIDS STUFF, learning to read and count.

3:30-4:00 IMAGINE THAT!, story time with FCPL librarians.

4:00-6:00 SILENT NETWORK, Emmy award-winning programs for the deaf and hearing-impaired.

6:00-6:30 LIBRARY BULLETIN BOARD

6:30-7:00 LIBRARY MAGAZINE and SERVICE FEATURES. *Career Moves, Your Business Consultant, & To Raise A Reader.*

7:00-7:30 VIRGINIA VOICES, interviews with authors.

7:30-8:30 PLANET EARTH, the geophysical world, concludes Sept. 24. ONLY ONE EARTH, a series on global ecology, begins Sept. 25.

8:30-9:30 THE GREAT PALACE, Britain's great houses, concludes Sept. 24. THE MIDDLE AGES, history and dramatization, begins Sept. 25.

9:30-10:00 CONNIE MARTINSON TALKS BOOKS, discussions with different authors each week.

10:00-11:00 THE STORY OF ENGLISH, concludes Sept. 10. IN SEARCH OF THE TROJAN WAR, with historian Michael Wood, begins Sept. 11.

the Library Channel on Media General Cable of Fairfax
For a free copy of the monthly program guide, call 790-8905.

Don't forget to register!

All programs are free, but space is limited.

Saturday, Sept. 23, 10:00
Women and Their Money, Part II. Ilene Lockman, Financial Education Center.

Tuesday, Sept. 26, 7:00
Wills and Estate Planning. Tom Martin, Financial Education Center.

Wednesday, Sept. 27, 7:30
Face the SATs with Confidence. For students and parents.

PATRICK HENRY
101 Maple Avenue East
Vienna * 938-0405
M,TH 1-9; TU,W 10-9; F 10-6; SA 9-5; SU 12-8

Saturdays, Sept. 2-30, 10:30
Saturday Family Films. No registration required.

Friday, Sept. 8, 10:00-3:00
Vienna Arts Society demonstration and exhibition.

Monday, Sept. 11, 7:15
Stress Management. Bonnie Brown, Adult Education.

Tuesdays, Sept. 12 & 19, 2:00
Fuzzies. Stories for age 3-5 with adult.

Tuesdays, Sept. 12-26, 10:30
Small One-ders. Stories for age 12-23 months with adult.

Wednesdays, Sept. 13-Oct. 11, 10:30
Thursdays, Sept. 14-Oct. 12, 2:00
If You're Happy and You Know It. Stories, fingerplays. Age 3-5.

Tuesdays, Sept. 19-Oct. 10, 7:00
Women and Their Money. Cosponsored by Financial Education Center.

Thursday, Sept. 21, 7:30
Vintage Radio. John Hickman, of WAMU radio station.

Monday, Sept. 25, 7:30
Your Dreams. Dream interpretation and recall. Rita Dwyer.

Thursday, Sept. 28, 11:00
Book Discussion. *Brave New World*, by Aldous Huxley.

Thursday, Sept. 28, 7:30
Stress. Dr. Dan Garfinkel.

POHICK
6450 Sydenstricker Road
Burke * 644-7333
M-TH 9-9; F 9-6; SA 9-5; SU 12-8

Tuesday, Sept. 5, 7:15
Discipline in the Preschool Years. Adult Education.

Wednesday, Sept. 13, 7:30
Friends of the Pohick Library. Public meeting.

Mondays, Sept. 18-Oct. 9, 3:30
Babysitting Class. Two-hour sessions, age 11 and up.

Monday, Sept. 18, 7:30
Basic Library Skills.

Tuesday, Sept. 19, 10:00 & 11:00
Behind the Wheel. Stories, rhymes and craft. Age 2-3 with adult.

Tuesday, Sept. 19, 7:15
Your Child's Self-Esteem. Adult Education.

Wednesday, Sept. 20, 9:45; 10:45
Tuesday, Sept. 26, 9:45; 10:45
Small One-ders. Stories and activities. Age 12-23 months with adult.

Wednesday, Sept. 20, 7:00
Small Business Start-ups. Cosponsored by Financial Education Center.

Thursday, Sept. 21, 10:30 & 1:30
Dog-Gone. Stories, rhymes and craft. Age 4 and 5.

Thursday, Sept. 21, 7:30
Kid's Connection. Flannelboard Stories for Preschoolers. Continues in October.

Monday, Sept. 25, 7:30
Culinary Hearts Kitchen. American Heart Association. Continues in October.

Tuesday, Sept. 26, 7:30
Coping with the Stress of Parenting Preschoolers.

Wednesday, Sept. 27, 10:30 & 1:30
Autumn Apples. Stories, rhymes, craft. Age 3-5 with adult.

Just arrived!

These new titles have just been added to the collection:

Forever Young: 20 Years Younger in 20 Weeks. A step-by-step rejuvenation program by Stuart Berger. 613B

The Evening Wolves. A complex portrait of a troubled family, by Joan Chase. FIC

Neon Bible. By John Kennedy Toole, Pulitzer Prize-winning author of *A Confederacy of Dunces.* FIC

The New Realities. Peter Drucker examines central issues of the next decade. 909.82D

The Summer People. A small community is disrupted by "summer people" in Marge Piercy's novel. FIC

Fall of the House of Hutton. Donna Carpenter recounts the Wall Street firm's tale of woe. 364.163C

READ

Loose-leaf Library

We all know that books burn, yet we have the greater knowledge that books cannot be killed by fire. People die, but books never die...Books are weapons...make them weapons for man's freedom.

...Franklin D. Roosevelt

Pohick, from page 5

Wednesday, Sept. 27, 7:30
Collecting Paperweights. Beverly Schindler.

Thursday, Sept. 28, 10:00 & 11:00
Autumn Animals. Stories, rhymes, craft. Age 2 with adult.

Thursday, Sept. 28, 7:30
Face the SATs with Confidence. For students and parents.

RESTON
11925 Bowman Towne Drive
Reston * 689-2700
M-TH 9-9; F 9-6; SA 9-5; SU 12-8

Tuesdays, Sept. 5-26, 9:30 & 10:30
Two's Company. Stories and activities. Age 2 with adult.

Tuesdays, Sept. 5-26, 1:00 & 2:00
Three's a Crowd. Stories and activities. Age 3.

Wednesday, Sept. 6, 7:30
Grief Education. By Northern Virginia Hospice. No registration.

Thursdays, Sept. 7-28, 1:00 & 2:00
Stories Plus. Stories and activities. Age 4-5.

Saturdays, Sept. 9-23, 10:30
Introduction to Smocking. Virginia Country Smockers. Limited enrollment.

Mondays, Sept. 11-25, 9:30; 10:30
Small One-ders. Stories and activities. Age 12-23 months with adult.

Monday, Sept. 11, 2:00
Anything Goes. Stories and activities. K-6 grade.

Tuesday, Sept. 12, 7:30
Strong Families, Competent Kids.

Wednesday, Sept. 13, 10:30
Book Discussion. *Portrait of the Artist as a Young Man,* by James Joyce.

Wednesday, Sept. 13, 10:00-2:00
50th Anniversary Reception. Also honors Reston Regional's 4th anniversary.

Wednesday, Sept. 13, 7:30
First Time Homeowners. No registration.

Monday, Sept. 18, 7:30
Face the SATs with Confidence. For students and parents.

Tuesday, Sept. 19, 7:00
Investment Planning for Retirement. Carol Goldstone, Financial Education Center.

RICHARD BYRD
7250 Commerce Street
Springfield * 451-8055
M,TH 1-9; TU,W 10-9; F 10-6; SA 9-5; SU Closed

Thursday, Sept. 7, 7:00
Decorating and Interior Design in the 1990s. Christine Sapienza.

Saturday, Sept. 9, 2:00
Face the SATs with Confidence. For students and parents.

Tuesday, Sept. 12, 7:30
How to Get a Job with the Fairfax County Public School System. FCPS Personnel Department.

Saturday, Sept. 16, 1:00
Introduction to Computer Genealogy. Survey of computers and programs for genealogical research.

Wednesday, Sept. 20, 7:30
Tips on Applications and Selection Process for Getting a Job with the County. County Personnel.

Wednesday, Sept. 27, 10:30
Time for Twos. Stories and fingerplays. Age 2 with adult.

Thursday, Sept. 28, 2:00
Anything Goes. Stories and fun. Age 3-5.

SHERWOOD
2501 Sherwood Hall Lane
Alexandria * 765-3645
M-TH 9-9; F 9-6; SA 9-5; SU 12-8

Tuesday, Sept. 5, 7:30
The Common Soldier in the American Civil War. Richard Galloway, author of *One Battle Too Many.*

Fridays, Sept. 8 & 29, 10:00
Friday, Sept. 15, 2:00
Reading and discussion of Shakespeare's *King Lear.* Elizabeth Chimento.

Mondays, Sept. 11-25, 10:00; 11:00
Time for Twos. Stories and activities. Age 2 with adult.

Monday, Sept. 11, 7:30
Face the SATs with Confidence. For students and parents.

Wednesdays, Sept. 13-27, 1:00
Bread and Butter Tales. Stories and activities. Age 3-4 with adult.

Wednesdays, Sept. 13-27, 2:00
Bread and Butter Tales. Stories and activities. Age 4-5.

Wednesday, Sept. 13, 7:15
How to Get Your First Byline. Rusti Evans, Adult Education.

Saturday, Sept. 23, 10:30
Goosey, Goosey, Gander. Nursery rhymes and songs. Age 12-23 months with adult.

Wednesday, Sept. 27, 7:30
Balancing Work and Family Responsibilities. Jane Thune.

THOMAS JEFFERSON
7415 Arlington Blvd.
Falls Church * 573-1060
M,TH 1-9; TU,W 10-9; F 10-6; SA 9-5; SU Closed

Tuesdays, Sept. 5 & 12, 10:30
Two for Twos. Stories, fingerplays and craft. Age 2 with adult.

Thursdays, Sept. 7-28, 2:00
Off We Go. Stories, songs and films. Age 3-5.

Tuesday, Sept. 19, 10:00
The Retirees Guide to Investments. Fredric Colby, Financial Education Center.

Tuesday, Sept. 19, 7:30
Tips for Buying a Personal Computer. Charles Hoover.

TYSONS-PIMMIT
7584 Leesburg Pike
Falls Church * 790-8088
M-TH 9-9; F 9-6; SA 9-5; SU 12-8

Thursday, Sept. 7, 7:00
How to Start Your Own Business. Tom Sides, consultant, and Larry Lindeman, attorney.

Wednesday, Sept. 13, 10:30
Wishes for Fishes. Stories, fingerplays, craft. Age 3-5.

Thursday, Sept. 14, 7:00
How to win a Federal Government Contract. James Arnn.

Wednesday, Sept. 20, 10:30
Rainbow Express. Stories, fingerplays, craft. Age 2 with adult.

Thursday, Sept. 21, 7:30
Image Update Workshop. Marybeth Rosato.

Monday, Sept. 25, 7:30
Face the SATs with Confidence. For students and parents.

WOODROW WILSON
6101 Knollwood Drive
Falls Church * 820-8774
M,TH 1-9; TU,W 10-9; F 10-6; SA 9-5; SU Closed

Thursday, Sept. 7, 7:15
Be Your Own Auto Mechanic. Prepare for winter. Cosponsored by Adult Education.

Tuesdays, Sept. 5 & 19, 11:00
Woodrow's Quilters. Stories about quilts for your children and grandchildren.

Don't forget!

All programs are free, but space is limited. Unless noted, registration is required, beginning two weeks before the scheduled event. To register, call your library.

Face the SATs with Confidence!

Prepare now for the SAT! In a free seminar this month, teacher-certified instructors offer proven strategies to help increase your self-confidence.

Learn how to:
- prepare for the exam
- pace yourself
- take on both verbal and math sections
- deal with the pressure

Free!

Programs offered by Centreville, Dolley Madison, Fairfax City Regional, George Mason Regional, Kings Park, Martha Washington, Pohick Regional, Reston Regional, Richard Byrd, Sherwood Regional, Tysons-Pimmit Regional

For exact days and times, see the individual branch listings in this issue. Limited registration, beginning two weeks before each program. Parents are welcome to attend.

September 1989 — page 8

Your appetite for literary trivia inspired this creation, with answers in next month's issue.

Feasts in Fiction

1 In this Washington-based *roman a clef*, a pregnant cookbook writer finds infidelity at home.

2 Breakfast of a different hue is a rhyming children's favorite.

3 A gargantuan gourmet detective and orchid fancier is the hero of 46 novels by a Chicago journalist.

4 Every season of the year is nice for eating this dish, title of a small book by a renowned illustrator.

5 According to the author, cornmeal pancakes are the favorite food of this Boston-based p.i. hero, with his own TV series.

6 A bear from Darkest Peru is always sticky from marmalade sandwiches, which he takes everywhere, even to the theatre.

7 A gypsy curse is embodied in a strawberry pie, and the American dream of losing weight becomes a nightmare.

8 Engaging Manhattan playgirl Holly Golightly cooks bizarre dishes, but longs to take her morning meal at a swanky jeweler's.

9 A favorite food is so enticing that Christopher Robin's friend gets stuck in a jar of it.

10 Chefs gathered to prepare a royal repast are coming to stylish ends, and a "bombe" goes off.

11 Teenagers are told to cool their ardor by going out for their favorite fast food.

12 Despite tips on cuisine and the best airline martini, life is no party for student cooks when a French boning knife becomes a murder weapon.

--Michele Leber

A celebration of reading and the written word, by one of America's premier artists. Full color posters commemorate the library's 50th anniversary. On sale now at all branches. Proceeds benefit the library's gift funds.

Fairfax County Public Library

This Month is published 12 times a year by the Office of Public Information, Fairfax County Public Library, 11216 Waples Mill Road, Fairfax, VA 22030. 703/246-5200.

© 1989, Fairfax County Public Library

Library Administration
11216 Waples Mill Road
Fairfax, Virginia 22030

BULK RATE
U.S. Postage
PAID
Permit No. 45
Fairfax, VA

Fairfax County Public Library 50th Anniversary, 1939-1989: "the past is prologue"